Faery Mysteries

The Strange & Obscure in Faeryland

JOHN KRUSE

GREEN MAGIC

GREEN MAGIC
53 Brooks Road
Street
Somerset
BA16 0PP
England

www.greenmagicpublishing.com

Designed and typeset by CARRIGBOY, Wells, UK
www.carrigboy.co.uk

ISBN 978-1-915580-00-9

GREEN MAGIC

Contents

Introduction

This book is concerned with the boundaries of faery. We will investigate the very limits of our understanding – and our definitions – of the faery folk. As we shall see, repeatedly – there are aspects of faery existence that still baffle our attempts to interpret and comprehend them, because they fail to adhere to ideas of a fixed nature and predictable behaviours that are encouraged by strict traditional scientific rationalism. Of course, there are aspects of modern physics which accept mutability and subjectivity, so perhaps faery nature isn't so strange after all.

What's more, time and again we shall see the problems of providing permanent labels and classifications. Certain faery types are hard to pin down, and can shift from category to category – sometimes seeming like faeries, but at other times like ghosts, or demons or monsters. This may feel frustrating, but it is part of the wonder of our rich folklore that should be embraced.

In this book, we will encounter a range of unfamiliar faeries. We shall discover those that act as witches' familiars and that bring dreams and nightmares; we shall explore the strange forms they can adopt, the surprising ways they move from place to place and – even – the odd games they play. British faerylore will prove to be even more surprising and mysterious than we may ever have supposed.

PART ONE

Obscure Faeries in the Denham List

Introduction

Michael Aislabie Denham (1801–1859) was an English merchant and collector of folklore. In the early part of his life, he conducted his business in Hull; later he set up as a general merchant at Piercebridge, County Durham. He collected all sorts of local lore – sayings, songs and folktales – much of which he self-published. After his death many of his works were collected together and republished by the newly established Folklore Society as 'The Denham Tracts.'

Denham recorded many valuable scraps of material. One of the most fascinating, found in the second volume of the *Tracts*, is a list of faeries and evil spirits. Denham drew upon a list already compiled by Reginald Scot in *The Discoverie of Witchcraft* (1584), perhaps supplementing this with another found in George Gascoigne's play *The Buggbears* (1565); he may even have drawn from one compiled by Thomas Hobbes in *Leviathan*, in which the philosopher mocked "The Absurd Opinion of Gentilisme" (in other words – pagans or non-Christians) whom, he said, had:

> "filled almost all places, with spirits called Daemons; the plains, with Pan, and Panises, or Satyres; the Woods, with Fawnes, and Nymphs; the Sea, with Tritons, and other Nymphs; every River, and Fountayn, with a Ghost of his name, and with Nymphs; every house, with it Lares, or Familiars; every man, with his Genius; Hell, with Ghosts, and spirituall Officers, as Charon, Cerberus, and the Furies; and in the night time, all places with Larvae, Lemures, Ghosts of men deceased, and a whole kingdome of Fayries, and Bugbears."[1]

---

1   T. Hobbes, *Leviathan,* 1651, c.12; for Scot, *Discoverie,* Book 7, c.15, see Part Two

To the resulting catalogue, Denham then added many additional terms of his own, to produce this encyclopaedic inventory.

"Grose observes, too, that those born on Christmas Day cannot see spirits; which is another incontrovertible fact. What a happiness this must have been seventy or eighty years ago and upwards, to those chosen few who had the good luck to be born on the eve of this festival of all festivals; when the whole earth was so overrun with ghosts, boggles, bloody-bones, spirits, demons, ignis fatui, brownies, bugbears, black dogs, spectres, shellycoats, scarecrows, witches, wizards, barguests, Robin-Goodfellows, hags, night-bats, scrags, breaknecks, fantasms, hob-goblins, hobhoulards, boggy-boes, dobbies, hob-thrusts, fetches, kelpies, warlocks, mock-beggars, mum-pokers, Jemmy-burties, urchins, satyrs, pans, fauns, sirens, tritons, centaurs, calcars, nymphs, imps, incubusses, spoorns, men-in-the-oak, hell-wains, fire-drakes, kit-a-can-sticks, Tom-tumblers, melch-dicks, larrs, kitty-witches, hobby-lanthorns, Dick-a-Tuesdays, Elf-fires, Gyl-burnt-tails, knockers, elves, raw-heads, Meg-with-the-wads, old-shocks, ouphs, pad-foots, pixies, pictrees, giants, dwarfs, Tom-pokers, tutgots, snapdragons, sprats, spunks, conjurers, thurses, spurns, tantarrabobs, swaithes, tints, tod-lowries, Jack-in-the-Wads, mormos, changelings, redcaps, yett-hounds, colt-pixies, Tom-thumbs, black-bugs, boggarts, scar-bugs, shag-foals, hodge-pochers, hob-thrushes, bugs, bull-beggars, bygorns, bolls, caddies, bomen, brags, wraithes, waffs, flay-boggarts, fiends, gallytrots, imps, gytrashes, patches, hob-and-lanthorns, gringes, boguests, bonelesses, Peg-powlers, pucks, fays, kidnappers, gally-beggars, hudskins, nickers, madcaps, trolls, robinets, friars' lanthorns, silkies, cauld-lads, death-hearses, goblins, hob-headlesses, buggaboes, kows or cowes, nickies, nacks, [necks] waiths, miffies, buckles, gholes, sylphs, guests, swarths, freiths, freits, gy-carlins [Gyre-carling], pigmies, chittifaces, nixies, Jinny-burnt-tails, dudmen, hell-hounds, dopple-gangers, boggleboes, bogies, redmen, portunes, grants, hobbits, hobgoblins, brown-men, cowies, dunnies, wirrikows, alholdes, mannikins, follets, korreds, lubberkins, cluricanns, kobolds, leprechauns, kors, mares, korreds, puckles, korigans, sjlvans, succubuses, black-men, shadows, banshees, lian-banshees, clabbernappers, Gabriel-hounds, mawkins, doubles, corpse lights or candles, scrats, mahounds, trows, gnomes, sprites, fates, fiends, sybils, nick-nevins, whitewomen, fairies, thrummy-caps, cutties and nisses, and apparitions of every shape, make, form, fashion, kind and description, that there was not a village in England that had not its own peculiar ghost. Nay, every lone tenement, castle, or mansion-house, which could boast of any antiquity had its bogle, its spectre, or its knocker. The churches, churchyards, and cross-roads, were all haunted. Every green lane had its boulder-stone on which an apparition kept watch at night. Every common had its circle of fairies belonging to it. And there was scarcely a shepherd to be met with who had not seen a spirit! [See *Literary Gazette*, December 1848, p.849]."[2]

This is a daunting catalogue, impressive (intimidating even) in its length and detail, and a little depressing in the sense that so many of the names now seem unfamiliar. It's clear how very rich the British faery tradition once was, and how much has been lost in the last two hundred years.

---

2 Denham's reference to the *Literary Gazette* is simply to an identical copy of the list that he submitted to the December 23rd issue of the journal (no.1666).

Parameters

Firstly, I want to edit and order Denham's rambling and sometimes repetitive list. Like Scot and Hobbes before him, he was quite undiscriminating in mixing up British and classical, faery and ghostly figures, which was perhaps done solely to end up with as long and as learned looking a catalogue as possible. It's possible to bring a greater sense of organisation to Denham's jumble of names, the result of which will be (I believe) a clearer sense of the nature of British faerydom.

I'll start by rejecting the words we know perfectly well and which I have described in detail in other books, like brownies, Robin Goodfellow and puck (and puckle), knockers, pixies, fays, elves, gnomes, changelings, the trows of Shetland and Orkney and many of the variations upon the word hob – the hobgoblins, hobthrusts and hobthrushes. Hob-thrust and thrush incorporate an element derived from the Old English for demon or giant. Denham's hob-houlard (sometimes seen as 'howlard') appears to be a compound with 'howlet' (owlet), thereby denoting a nocturnal goblin. With these faery names should be included Denham's 'ouph.' This word is simply a variant of elf and it will also be encountered as aulf, owf, oof and, of course, oaf. Today it means a foolish or stupid person; this connotation derived from the earlier sense of a changeling, an elf that had been substituted for a child and which was perceived to be mentally disabled.

I'll also reject from consideration all the foreign and/or classical material: the satyrs, pans, fauns, fates, sirens, lars, tritons, centaurs, and nymphs; the continental dwarves, kobolds, korrigans, foletti, and trolls; the Irish leprechauns, lian-banshees (apparently Denham's own compound of lhiannan shee and banshee) and clurichauns. There are also a number of general magical or spirit related terms included that we can safely ignore:

sybils, wizards and witches. Quite a few names for the devil have also been excluded from the discussion, such as mahound (a medieval derivation from Mohammed), as have a range of words that seem to denote demons or evil spirits, such as freiths and freits and mares (as in nightmares, which we will deal with in Part Two).

There's a class of ghostly or ghoulish being included in the list that doesn't really belong with faeries and goblins. These are the ghouls and phantasms, as well as the fetches (the spirit or double of a dying person), which are also called swaithes, swarths, wraithes, waffs, waiths and dopplegangers. Although there is a definite crossover between apparitions of the dead and Faery, these entities are distinct from faeries. Denham's 'death-hearses' and corpse lights or candles belong in this category too. The death-hearses and hell-wains are what we'd call headless coachmen today, I think, although it's worth noting in passing that 'Hellwain' was used as the name of a witch's familiar by Christopher Middleton in his play *The Witch*, appearing in a speech by Hecate which makes direct allusion to the notorious trial of the witches of St Osyth in Essex in 1582. Other familiars invoked in this scene are Puckle and Robin (see the earlier paragraph and Part Five) and Pidgen, who strongly echoes the faery Pigwiggen in Drayton's *Nymphidia*.[1]

Other ghost-like apparitions include scrags, break-necks, spectres, sprats (spirits or sprites) and kitty-witches. With these I have included the northern 'silkies' and 'cauld-lads', although in fact these ghost-like beings can be hybrid creatures, possessing several of the characteristics of brownies as well as sometimes acting as a guardian in spirit or, conversely, as a bogle. The best-known silky is that of Black Heddon in Northumberland and the most famous Cauld Lad was the one found at Hilton in the same county.

---

1 Middleton, *The Witch*, Act I, scene 2.

Denham also included in his inventory the names of supernatural creatures that very evidently aren't faeries. There are the giants, but also the snapdragons and fire-drakes. Fire-breathing serpents plainly don't have any place in Faery.

A few final odds and ends remain. Denham's word 'tutgot' is not a noun, but an adjective; according to James Orchard Halliwell, it means someone who has been come upon, overtaken or seized and possessed by a 'tut,' a sort of Lincolnshire goblin. Despite Denham's mention of the term, it seems to have had only a limited currency, being used in and near Spilsby in Lincolnshire – rather, even, than in all parts of that county. 'Tom-tit' would appear to be a related hob-goblin, whom we shall meet again in Part Five.[2]

It would look from a few entries as though Denham also included some insults or derogatory terms. A hudskin is a foolish or clownish fellow (in the Lincolnshire dialect); perhaps it's in the list for the same reason that madcaps and patches were included. A clabbernapper appears to be nothing more than a gossip; a 'scrat' is a Northern dialect term for a hermaphrodite. However, 'Old Scrat (or Skrat)' is also a Lancashire sprite, who will appear in empty carts and make them very heavy and difficult to move. He was known for this trick at Brindle, near Leyland, either stopping carts or making it nearly impossible for the horses to pull them. Then, one time, he unwisely leapt on a hearse and stopped it, as a result of which he was laid forever by the local vicar. The name was once also used to scare children in the North of England: "By god! but auld Scratty'll git thi if thoo doesn't come in!"[3]

There are some Scots beings in the list, such as the hags, nick-nevin and the gyre carlin. Scottish Gaelic creatures also appear, which include kelpies, shellycoats (a Lowland fresh-water bogle),

---

2 J.L. Brogden, *Provincial Words ... Current in Lincolnshire*, 1866, 214; J.O. Halliwell, *A Dictionary of Archaic & Provincial Words*, 1889, vol.2.
3 T. Wilkinson, 'On the Popular Customs of Lancashire, Part 2,' *Transactions of the Historic Society of Lancashire & Cheshire*, vol.12, 1859–60, 95; Wright, *Rustic Speech & Folklore*, 198.

banshees and *lhiannan-shees* (the faery lovers whom we'll examine in Part Two). This more sexual sort of supernatural also includes the incubus and succubus, as will be discussed.[4]

With this pruning performed, we can then start to sort out the list that remains. Pre-industrial Britain was teeming with supernatural beings – as we can tell – and Denham was possibly right to pity the person who possessed the second sight and who would have been afflicted by visions of such hosts of faeries and goblins on all sides. He mentioned that those born at Christmas would have had this ability, but other days or times of day are also auspicious, such as Sundays or early in the morning.

---

4 For more detail see my *Beyond Faery* and *Who's Who in Faeryland.*

Boggarts and Bogles

A large number of goblin-like beings is included in Denham's list, their main attribute being terrifying travellers and those visiting certain locations. Sir Walter Scott characterised these creatures very well as "freakish spirit[s], who delight rather to perplex and frighten mankind than either to serve or seriously to hurt them." They include boggles, bugbears, boggy-boes, boggleboes, bogies, bugs, bull-beggars, bygorns, bolls, caddies, bomen, boguests, buckles, buggaboes, black-bugs, cutties (female bogles, from Scotland and the Border region), hobhoulards, tints, hodge-pokers, alholds, swarths and black-men (dark entities), mormos, dudmen (deadmen or scarecrows) and scar-bugs. One thing that Denham's enumeration emphasises is the fact that the element 'bug' or 'bogey' is particularly applied to these beings – and not just in English, but in Welsh, Gaelic and many other Indo-European languages as well. What we can't be certain about is how very different these many sprites may have been: Denham has indiscriminately thrown together names taken from all over Britain. Many are very local, meaning that substantially fewer actual types of bogey may have been identified by our ancestors than this long tally suggests.

It's important to appreciate that the terminology in the list is not – and obviously cannot be – scientifically precise. For example, Denham's 'flay-boggarts' are really a sort of domesticated spirit like a brownie or hobgoblin. They are labelled boggarts, whom we would normally regard as unfriendly, yet they live and work on farms, receiving food and drink in return for their considerable labours. Their willingness to undertake the hardest chores, such as threshing grain, is reflected in the name: the 'flay-boggart' is simply one of the species, equipped with a flail, at work in the barn. By contrast, mormos were described as a sort of spectre by James Halliwell, who cited Jeremy Collier's *Short View of the English Stage*: "One would think by this [that] the devils were mere mormos and bugbears, fit only to fright children and fools." Similarly, the 'alhold' has been defined as a goblin whilst the boll is an 'apparition.'[1]

Another special category of boggart may be the phantasmal beasts that appear to terrify users of the highway or near certain landmarks such as churches and old houses. Amongst these are the numerous black dogs, barguests, old-shocks, pad-foots, pictrees and brags, shag-foals, kows or cowes, gytrashes, grants, gallytrots and gally-beggars. The element 'gally' seen in the last two names means to frighten; the earlier 'cow' probably has the same sense, as in the modern 'cowed.' All of the creatures included in this list will appear at night in the form of hounds, calves, cows, donkeys, horses and large shaggy dark beasts of uncertain genus. One habit of these barguests and boggarts, for example, is to leap onto the shoulders of night-time travellers riding them like horses for a distance and thoroughly scaring them. This habit echoes that of the nightmare that we shall examine in Part Two. The black hounds just mentioned need to be distinguished from those types of hound that fly through the air and often foretell or mark a death. These include Denham's Gabriel-hounds, yett-hounds and hell-hounds.[2]

Once again, the terms applied to this group of 'faery beasts' indicate a varied assessment of their fundamental nature. The pictree has been labelled a ghost whilst the 'trash' element of gy or guy-trash derives from the Anglo-Saxon *thyrs*, which originally meant a giant or demon (the same word that appears in Denham's hobthrush and hobthrust). What must be constantly appreciated is the looseness of definitions. Supernatural beings

---

1 J.O. Halliwell, *A Dictionary of Archaic & Provincial Words*, 1889, two volumes; Collier, *Short View of the English Stage*, 1698, 192.

2 Wright, *Rustic Speech*, 193; I examine all of these bogies and faery beasts in detail in my *Beyond Faery* (2020).

could hover, as it were, between different classes of supernatural entity, requiring that we approach their study without being too dogmatic and with an open and enquiring mind.[3]

3 J.O. Halliwell, *A Dictionary of Archaic & Provincial* Words; C.P.G. Scott, 'The Devil & His Imps,' *Transactions of the American Philological Association,* vol. 26, 1895, 131.

Wills of the Wisp

The phenomenon of the spirit light or *ignis fatuus* that leads people out of their way at night, getting them lost or luring them into bogs, is well-known across Britain and has attracted a variety of colourful local names. Denham uncovered many different names for these: hobby-lanthorns, Dick-a-Tuesdays, elf-fires, Gyl-burnt-tails, kit-a-can-sticks, Jinny-burnt-tails, Jack-in-the-Wads, friars' lanthorns, Meg-with-the-wads, hob-and-lanthorns, spunks and Jemmy-burties. Another such is Peggy wi' t' Lantern, seen in marshy places and sikes in Yorkshire and Derbyshire.

All these personal names indicate the clear perception that it is individual sprites who are maliciously creating these misleading lights for the specific purpose of tormenting a particular nocturnal traveller.[1]

---

1 S.O. Addy, *Household Tales*, 1895, 138; see too my *Beyond Faery* (2020), c.12.

Nursery and Cautionary Sprites

This category of creatures exists mainly to scare incautious or recalcitrant children into behaving better and/or staying away from dark, dangerous places around the home, such as cupboards and roof-spaces, or perilous locations outside like ponds, wells and riverbanks.

The group includes a number of so-called 'nursery' or domestic sprites, such as bloody-bones, raw-heads, Knocky-Boh, Tom-pokers, Tom-dockins, hob-headlesses, mum-pokers, bonelesses and tod-lowries, as well as sprites who guard orchards and nut groves, amongst whom we reckon the melch-dicks and colt-pixies. The exact nature of these beings is open for debate. To use an example not cited by Denham, in Cheshire around Macclesfield children used to be alarmed with stories of Jonny Cobler. He pushed a barrow full of firewood around the streets – and misbehaving children might be taken away by him too. Informants have described him as a boggart, but goblin, bogie – or some other term – might be as apt.[1]

NURSERY SPRITES

Several of these beings have just been identified. Tod-lowery is a hob-goblin whose imminent appearance is used to alarm infants. The two elements of the name both mean a 'fox,' but combined together they have acquired a new, supernatural sense in the area of Lincolnshire and the Fens. A related being is Tom or Tommy-

---

1 See the general discussion of this topic in *Round About Our Coal Fire,* c.2.

loudy, a name used in Holderness for a loud blustering goblin who shakes the window-panes, whistles and moans through the lattice, scaring children with his noise.[2]

Interestingly, though, the fenland folklorist Mrs Balfour classed the tod-lowries along with witches and seemed to regard them as rather more serious and dangerous than mere nursery sprites. She described the charm that protected against them being used by adult men; it involved reciting the 'Our Father' backwards and then spitting towards the east.[3]

Knocky-boh is a North Yorkshire bogie who taps behind the wainscot panels to frighten children. Faery authority Katherine Briggs remarked that the being seemed to be a kind of boggart, or even a poltergeist. Mumpoker is known on the Isle of Wight and is used to frighten small children: "I'll zend the mumpoker ater ye." The 'mum' element of the name denotes his silent and stealthy approach as he creeps up on the little ones, the word being related most probably to the phrase 'to keep mum.' That said, one etymologist suggested a plausible link to the German word *mummel,* a bugbear. Hodge Poker appears to be a related sprite, but his nature is now obscure. He's been described as a "a goblin of perished fame" and, other than his lurking habit, little can be said about him. He seems to be an inhabitant of Faery, as John Florio's Italian-English dictionary of 1611 defined 'folletto' as "a hobgoblin, an elfe, a Robin-good-fellow, a hodge poker." However, the first element 'Hodge' derives from the name Roger, which was used familiarly of the devil.[4]

Tom Dockin is another Yorkshire bogie. He is equipped iron teeth, with which he devours bad children. The element 'Dockin'

2 Brogden, *Provincial Words… Current in Lincolnshire*, 1866; M. A. Streatfeild, *Lincolnshire and the Danes*, 1884, 373; see too *County Folklore*, vol.5 & Wright, *Rustic Speech*, 198; Ross, Stead & Holderness, *Holderness Gloss*, 1877, 149.
3 Balfour, 'Legends of the Cars,' *Folklore*, vol.2, 1891, 153, 'The Tiddy Mun.'
4 Wright, *Rustic Speech*, 198; Smith, *Isle of Wight Words*, 1881, 22; Wedgwood, *Dictionary of English Etymology*, 1859–62; Scott, 'The Devil & His Imps,' *Transactions of the American Philological Association*, 110.

in this name is very likely to derive from the verb 'to dock,' meaning to cut. Tom-poker is a closely related East Anglian bogie who is "the great bugbear and terror of naughty children" inhabiting dark closets, holes under stairs, unoccupied cock-lofts and such like. He lies in wait in these so-called 'poker holes' for unsuspecting infants who trespass there. An anonymous tract from 1673 describes how Tom Poker "scares Children in the Country, and cries don't go to London, for [he] will get you and put you into his Pocket." A century later, in *Tommy Thumb's Song Book*, 'Nurse Lovechild' declared "This in particular, I insist on ... that you never mention a Bull Beggar, Tom Poker, Raw Head and Bloody Bones ...".[5]

The 'poker' element in the names of both Mumpoker and Tom Poker denotes a hobgoblin or bogie – hence "A mother when her child is wayward ... scareth it with some pocar or bull-begger." The term derives from an older word, pocar or pocker, which meant a devil. This in turn produced the obsolete adjective 'pokerish,' which was applied to localities or circumstances suggestive of ghosts or fearful things. The forename 'Tom' which was applied to both Tom Dockin and Tom Poker comes from another familiar name for the devil, 'Old Tom.' Pokey-hokey, from East Anglia and Punky, from West Yorkshire, would appear to be very similar entities.[6]

As will be seen from this section – as well as that which follows – the dividing lines between faeries, goblins, bogies and demons are uncertain. The terminology is fluid and must reflect a flexibility in people's perceptions of these creatures. They are liminal beings, not subject to fixed or stable definitions.

---

5 Wright, *Rustic Speech*, 198; Briggs, *Dictionary of Fairies*, 256; R. Forby, *Vocabulary of East Anglia*, 1830; Scott, 'The Devil & His Imps,' *Transactions of the American Philological Association*, 142; *Remarks upon Remarques* 98; *Tommy Thumb's Song Book*, 1788, vol.5.

6 Arthur Dent, *The Plain Man's Pathway to Heaven*, 1601, 109; Scott, 'The Devil & His Imps,' *Transactions of the American Philological Association*, 126 & 85.

RAWHEAD & BLOODYBONES

Around the disused coal pits of the Staffordshire Black Country, both rawhead and bloody bones were known as half human, half animal beings. They were very dangerous, but would periodically come out of the pits to beg for food and other items at nearby cottages. By late Victorian times, however, they had diminished to not much more than bugbears used by parents to scare their children away from playing too near to the pit mouths. In the north of England, Tommy Rawhead and his companions would lurk near ponds, streams and flooded marl pits.[7]

These two bogies are seldom separated and their identities, appearances and habits tended to merge. Rawhead (sometimes also called Rawflesh) is portrayed as a being with a skull head or a flayed body; bloodybones' looks speak for themselves. From at least the mid-sixteenth century, they have been regarded as creatures suitable for scary stories told to small children. For example, in 1566 John Rastell wrote about a "Grandmother's tale of Bloudy Bones, Raw head, Bloudelesse and Ware woulf." Philosopher Ralph Lever explained in 1573 how some "Wordes ... signifie matters which are not in deede, but are fained to be, as Hobthrusts, rawhed, purgatorie."[8]

Bloody-bones is another creature primarily used to thrill or scare children. In the *Wyll of the Devyll* (1548) he is seen as one of Satan's servants, whose last will and testament is to be "written by our faithful secretaries, Hobgoblin, Rawhed and Bloodybones, in the spiteful audience of all the court of hell." Generally, though, this sprite is treated as a more mundane spirit, akin to a goblin. Thus, lexicographer John Florio describes the "mani imagined spirits that nurces fraie their babies withal, to make them leave crying, as we say bugbear, or else rawe head and

7 C.S. Burne, 'Staffordshire Folk & Their Lore,' *Folklore*, vol.7, 1896, 371; Wright, *Rustic Speech & Folklore*, 198.
8 Rastell, *Third Book, Beware of M Jewel*, 1566, fo.9; Lever, *Art of Reason*, I, x, 48.

bloodie bone." It's hard to imagine why these creatures would make infants calm down: for surely, as the playwrights Fletcher and Massinger understood, the response is almost certain to be the exact opposite: "But now I looke like bloodybone and raw head, to fright children."[9]

These nursery sprites could be very effective. John Locke described "the usual method of servants to awe children, and keep them in subjection, by telling them of rawhead and bloodybones, and such other Names, as carry them the Ideas of some hurtful, terrible Things, inhabiting darkness." The terrifying memories of those childhood nightmares could persist into adulthood, as Henry Brooke suggested in *The Fool of Quality:* "I should not like, even now, to have my curtains at midnight opened suddenly upon me by a death's head and bloody bones."[10]

Over time, the names of these two horrific creatures became more and more synonymous.[11] Moreover, they were more and more employed in everyday speech to denote any threat or proposal that was being deliberately set up to alarm and dismay people. The pair's names were used in this sense in respect of opponents' political or economic arguments throughout the eighteenth and nineteenth centuries. Nonetheless, the original meaning was not wholly forgotten – as James Joyce demonstrated in 1922, writing in *Ulysses* of "The corpse chewer! Raw Head and Bloodybones!"[12]

9 *Wyll of Devyll,* 1548, sig.C iv; E. Settle, *City Ramble,* 1711, IV, 55; J. Florio, *World of Wordes,* 1598; Fletcher & Massinger, *The Prophetesse,* 1640, IV, 5.

10 John Locke, *Some Thoughts Concerning Education,* 1693, 131, 158; H. Brooke, *The Fool of Quality,* 1766, I, iii, 81.

11 See, for example, *Leveller,* 1659, 4; T. Morton, *New English Canaan,* 1637, III, xxv, 170; J. F. Bernard, *Praise of Hell,* 1760, I, xiii, 131; *Life of N. Frowde,* 1773, 19; Leigh Hunt, *Indicator,* Dec.22nd 1819, 81.

12 Joyce, *Ulysses,* II, 541.

WATER SPRITES

Denham enumerated quite a few fresh water spirits, living in rivers and pools. These include Peg-powlers, nisses and nixies, nickies and nacks. The last four are all, pretty clearly, related and will be discussed separately a little later.

The 'white women' Denham mentioned frequently are spirits believed to be female that haunt springs and wells. Jenny or Jinny Greenteeth lurked at the bottom of stagnant pools in Cheshire and the North West, waiting to pull down careless children. In Lancashire, Jenny might be joined by Bloodybones and 'Old Nick' (see later) in terrorising children around pools and beside rivers. Deep water shaded by low hanging willow branches was believed to be a spot particularly favoured by her.[13]

The creatures that Denham enumerated are, in fact, just a handful of the many like entities found across the British Isles. There's Mary Hosies in southern Scotland, Jenny the Whinney on the Isle of Man, Star Nell in the north-west of England and many more. Once again, we see the tendency to give familiar names to murderous beings.

GUARDIANS OF CROPS

English orchards and nut groves are haunted by sprites whose role is both to bring life and fertility to the trees and to protect the fruit from thefts. The faeries go by various regional names, including Jack up the Orchard, the grig and the apple tree man. The first of them, Jack, in Shropshire at least had a more general role of keeping children in check, hence the threat "If yo' dunna tak' car' I'll shewn yo' Jack-up-the-orchut."[14]

---

13 T. Wilkinson, 'On the Popular Customs of Lancashire, Part 2,' *Transactions of the Historic Society of Lancashire & Cheshire*, vol.12, 1859–60, 95; R. Holland, *A Glossary of Words Used in the County of Chester*, 1886, 182; Darlington, *Folk-speech of South Cheshire*, 1887, 233.

14 Wright, *Rustic Speech & Folklore*, 198.

These protective or cautionary roles notwithstanding, these spirits appear to be inseparable from the trees they protect, so that thinking of them as indwelling may be a more accurate way of conceiving of them. Ceremonies used to be conducted in winter to 'wassail the trees' with libations of cider so as to encourage their growth. At harvest time in Somerset a few apples would always be left behind on the trees, which would be regarded as pixie-property. This customary offering was called 'pixying,' 'grigging' or the 'pixy-hoarding' and in return it was hoped that the next year's crop would be blessed. The traditional Yuletide rituals address the 'old apple tree,' but surely this must denote not the mere organism but a life or spirit within it. The autumn gifts of apples far more explicitly acknowledge the vital faery presence in the trees. A Somerset proverb, "So many cratches [baskets], so many cradles" explicitly links fertility in the orchards and groves to fertility and growth in the human population.[15]

Fruit tree spirits are found across England. One writer listed the following:

"Churn-milk Peg (West Yorkshire & Malham, North Yorkshire) and Melsh Dick (north country) are wood-demons supposed to protect soft, unripe nuts from being gathered by naughty children, the former being wont to beguile her leisure by smoking a pipe. The Gooseberry-wife (Isle of Wight), in the guise of a large furry caterpillar, takes charge of the green gooseberries, hence 'If ye goos out in the gearden, the gooseberry-wife'll be sure to ketch ye'; while in the orchards is Awd Goggie (East Yorkshire), guarding the unripe apples."

Another writer described Awd Goggie as a wicked sprite and added that children are warned to stay away from orchards at "improper times" otherwise (just like the gooseberry wife)

15 See Homer Sykes, *Once a Year*, 1977; R. Tongue, *Somerset Folklore*, 1965, 119; see also my *Faery*, 2020, chapter 5.

"Awd Goggie is seer [sure] to get em." We can also add to this list Nut Nan, who guards the hazels from theft with threats of burning naughty children with heated pokers. Churn-milk Peg, meanwhile, is described as being an old and very ugly hag, whose name derives from the hazelnuts in their green state, when they're called 'churn-milk'. All she says is "Smoke! smoke a wooden pipe!/ Getting nuts before they're ripe!" and if this doesn't work, she'll abduct the disobedient youths. Melsh Dick apparently derives his name from the same unripe, 'mushy' or 'mulchy' nuts; he too will make off with disobedient children.[16]

All of these northern sprites were assisted by Clap-Cans, a being with no form or substance whose sole purpose is to scare away youngsters by beating on tins or cans with sticks. So, in 1874, one writer described how, in the recent past, "few of the lonely, out-of-the-way places – the wells, the bypaths, the dark old lanes and solitary houses – escaped the reputation of being haunted by boggarts, feeorin [things that cause fear], witches, fairies, clap-cans and such like beings of terror, who were supposed to be lurking in almost every retired corner and sombre looking place...". For example, near Bury in Lancashire there was a pasture called Downbottoms that used to be haunted by clap-cans, who would scare solitary travellers and trap children. It would lure cows with a sound like the jingling of milk pails, with a view to drinking their milk.[17]

In the south of England, Lazy Lawrence haunted orchards from Hampshire to Somerset. In the former it seems that, rather like the colt-pixy or cole-pexy in Dorset, he might take the form of a horse and chase naughty children and apple thieves.[18] In Somerset, Lawrence inflicted crippling ailments on anyone

---

16 Wright, *Rustic Speech & Folklore*, 198; Gutch, *County Folklore (East Yorkshire)*, vol. 6, 40; Ross, Stead & Holderness, *Holderness Glossary*, 1877, 68.

17 Wright, *Rustic Speech & Folklore*, 194; 'Wassail, or Christmas Eve in a County Inn,' *Manchester Times*, Dec.19th 1874, 1; 'Peel family – Its Rise & Fortunes, c.9,' *Manchester Times*, Nov.2nd 1850, 3.

18 Brand, *Popular Antiquities*, vol.2, 512–513.

detected stealing the fruit. One spell used by farmers to protect their crops wished on the intruders that:

> "Starke be their sinews ...
> May dread and doubt
> Enclose them about ...
> So be the cramp in the toes
> Cramp and crooking
> And fault in their footing."[19]

The thieves would become immobile and trapped, hence the rhyme "Lazy Laurence, let me goo/ Don't hold me summer and winter too."

As already remarked, these orchard spirits are often classed as 'nursery sprites' because of their particular role in stopping children 'scrumping' fruit and nuts before they are ready to be picked. Whilst this function was doubtless an important one, as it both protected the crops and avoided infants getting poorly eating unripe produce, it's clear that these spirits may also partake of the nature of fertility and tree spirits too.[20]

---

19 British Library Add MS 36674 or J.O. Halliwell, *Popular Rhymes & Nursery Tales,* 273–274.

20 See too my *Faeries & the Natural World* (2021).

Other Names in Denham's List

As readers will have seen, Denham's list of supernatural beings is full of names and words that are entirely unfamiliar today. I shall examine a number in detail.

DUNNIES

Dunnies are ambivalent beings who are found on the Scottish borders, and especially Northumberland. They can manifest as small brownie-like beings, but they seldom do anything helpful for human households. Instead, they will overturn furniture at night, swap babies for changelings or cause nuisance when bringing midwives to births.[1]

The most famous is the Hazlerigg Dunnie which has been known to take the form of a horse in order to trick a rider into mounting him, before galloping off and then either disappearing from under the victim or tipping the horseman in a bog. The dunnie is also said to disguise itself as a plough-horse, only to vanish when the ploughman takes him into the stable.[2]

In a cave in the Cockenheugh Hills, and on Fowberry Bridge (both near Wooler in Northumberland), another form of the dunny appears that is said to have been either a former Border reiver or a suicide (or possibly both of these). This ghostlike creature is seen as a dun-coloured horse or donkey which scours the area in search of its lost treasure and may sometimes be seen sitting on the edge of a quarry, enjoying the fresh air.[3]

---

1 Balfour, *County Folklore,* vol.4, *Printed Extracts,* no.4, Northumberland, 14.
2 W. Henderson, *Notes on the Folklore of the Northern Counties,* 1879, 263.
3 'Sprites of Northumberland & Durham,' *Newcastle Courant,* April 2nd, 1880, 6.

DOBBY

The dobby or dobie is a being who is – and isn't – familiar. On the one hand, Dobbs and Dobby are local names in Sussex and in Yorkshire and Lancashire for the brownie or domestic hob. The name seems to be derived from Old Hob or Hobby and denotes "a person marked by some physical or mental peculiarity, an awkward, clumsy man, a stupid fellow, a simpleton, a fool." It was used to refer in a familiar manner to both devils and goblins.[4]

Though naturally lazy, for favoured individuals at special times the dobby will exert himself incredibly, helping with farm and household chores and completing major tasks in one night – hence the Sussex saying 'Master Dobbs has been helping you.' However, he is also over-prone to mischievous pranks, such as playing noisily in the kitchen at night or jumping up behind lone horsemen who are out late and squeezing them, sometimes terrifying them to death. This perhaps makes the dobby more like Robin Goodfellow or Puck than the usual faithful brownie. However, with the spelling 'dobie' he is a sprite of the most northerly English counties and the Borders – related to the brownie, but less intelligent. Being slower and more gullible than a brownie, a dobie is seen as poor second choice to undertake a task.[5]

The name is also used for a ghost. This may be a family ghost, as at Morthan Tower, Rokeby, where the spirit of a murdered woman haunted the house, or at Crosby Ravensworth Hall in Westmorland, where it guarded treasure buried under the old medieval tower. When the tower was demolished, the dobby left – but only after informing the resident of the hall where the

---

4 C.P.G. Scott, 'The Devil & His Imps,' *Transactions of the American Philological Association*, vol. 26, 1895, 79 & 88.

5 Wright, *Rustic Speech & Folklore*, 1913, 201–202; R. Willan, 'A List of Ancient Words at Present Used in the Mountainous District of the West Riding of Yorkshire,' *Archaeologia Cambrensis*, vol.17, 1814, 144; W. Henderson, *Notes on the Folklore of the Northern Counties*, 1879, 209; H. Aitken, *A Forgotten Heritage*, 1973, 27.

treasure was to be found. This sort of dobby is commemorated in literature, for instance in Washington Irving's *Bracebridge Hall* – "An ancient grange … supposed … to be haunted by a dobbie" – and in Sir Walter Scott's *Peveril* – "The Dobby's Walk was within the inhabited domains of the Hall."[6]

The name dobie or dobby is also applied to ghosts haunting other sites, such as the Ealinghearth Dobby, which is found between Newby Bridge and the lane at Fearing Brow in Cumbria. The dobby here is seen as a white apparition which will scare travellers with strange sounds and by jumping up onto passing carts to ride for a short distance. At Bardsea, on the Cumbrian coast near Barrow, another white dobby is seen on stormy nights, walking mournfully along a road with a white hare with bloodshot eyes. The spectral pair will also appear in the church at night if the bell is being tolled.[7]

To add a final layer of confusion, Bridgegate in Barnard Castle, County Durham, is haunted at nights by a large black dog dragging a chain. This is called the 'Briggate Dobie' yet it has been classed as a barguest. In a similar fashion, Sir Walter Scott regarded the Rokeby dobie and others as types of family barguests – hence, in *Rob Roy* the author wrote "He needed not to care for ghaist or barghaist, devil or dobbie."[8]

MEN-IN-THE-OAK

There are scattered traditional references to this class of faery being. Whether they are a separate class, or just an alternative name for faeries found living in oak woods, is not clear. The 'pucks' were known to have frequented such forests, for example,

---

6 W. Irving, *Bracebridge Hall*, 1822, xvi, 136; Scott, *Peveril*, 1823, I, ix, 231.

7 Bowker, *Goblin Tales of Lancashire*, 152.

8 *Northern Echo, Jan. 1st 1894, 3*; W. Henderson, *Notes on the Folklore of the Northern Counties*, 1879, 209, fn.1, citing Scott's *Rokeby* Canto 2 and *Letters on Demonology & Witchcraft*, no.3.

but more recently the oak-men have emerged as an independent faery tribe, as in Beatrix Potter's *Fairy Caravan* (1929).[9]

REDCAPS

Wearing a red cap is a tell-tale sign of a faery across the British Isles, but when Denham included this being in his list he was surely thinking of the 'redcap' of the Scottish Borders, a malevolent goblin said to lurk in ruins and to dye its headwear in the blood of its victims.[10]

'Old Red Cap' is just such a being, commemorated by the poet William Scott Irving in his poem 'Fair Helen' (1814). He haunts Blackett Tower on the Borders and, at the "unholy hour" of midnight, "Red Cap wakes his eldritch cry ...". At Hermitage Castle in Roxburghshire, another redcap, also called Red-comb or Bloodycap, although prone to draining travellers' blood at night, or scooping out their brains, also served the magician Lord Soulis, guarding his master's treasure long after he had been caught and executed.[11]

Although the redcap is generally localised in the very south of Scotland, there is a being known from Moray that sounds almost identical. The small loch called Lochan-Nan-Deaan, near Tomintoul, is haunted by a small man in a red cap, whose roar can shake the surrounding hills and who can make the lake's waters boil and turn red. The little man was known for having a taste for human flesh.[12]

TOM-THUMBS

In the seventeenth century Tom Thumb was a small elf well-known to people in ballads and rhymes. Since then, he has been

---

9   See my *Fairy Ballads*.
10 W. Henderson, *Notes on the Folklore of the Northern Counties*, 1879, 253.
11 Westwood & Kingshill, *Lore of Scotland*, 126 & 246–247.
12 See also my *Beyond Faery* (2020) c.8.

caught up by romance and fairy-tale and has lost almost all his supernatural nature. Denham treats Tom as a class of faery being; it's doubtful whether this was ever the case.[13]

HOBBITS

Denham gives us a fascinating and isolated mention of these beings. We know nothing more about them from British tradition, but a sharp-eyed young literature professor in Oxford spotted the word at some point during the 1930s, and the rest is history. Many have claimed that Tolkien devised this name, but it is demonstrably not true. The exact nature of Denham's 'hobbit' is a mystery, but the word was also used to denote a small measure of grain and may have a Welsh origin. Alternatively, it may be derived from or be a diminutive of the much more familiar hob or hobgoblin. A 'hobbety-hoy' denoted a youth between boy – and man-hood, rather appropriate for the hobbits of Tolkien's tales.[14]

REDMEN

These are small, solitary elves of Northamptonshire, often found living near wells or in dells. They will come to beg for food from humans and, if one is caught, he can then be made to lead his captor to his hidden hoard of gold.[15]

CADDIES

A term from Yorkshire, it is the diminutive of the rare cad(d) – a spirit. In John Hutton's *A Tour to the Caves, in the Environs of Ingleborough and Settle* (1781), caddy is given as a word for a

---

13 See my discussion of this in *Fayerie and Who's Who in Faeryland*.
14 For a full discussion, see Donald O'Brien, 'On the Origin of the Name "Hobbit",' *Mythlore* vol.16, no.2 (winter 1989).
15 Sternberg, *Dialect & Folklore of Northamptonshire*, 142 & 196–7; Hill, *Folklore of Northamptonshire*, 152.

ghost or bugbear. It is very clearly a sort of supernatural being, as two examples will show. "One of these cadds or familiars still knocking over their pillow," was used by Francis Osborne in his *Advice to a Son*, (1656), whilst "Rebellion wants no cad nor elfe/ But is a perfect witchcraft of itself," appears in 'Elegies' by Stuart poet Henry King.[16]

CALCARS

Mentioned by both Reginald Scot in *The Discoverie of Witchcraft* (1584) and by Denham, the word appears to derive from the verb *calculare*. Halliwell's *Dictionary of Archaic & Provincial Words* defines 'calcar' as an astrologer, 'to calke' being to calculate or to cast a figure or birth chart. In John Bale's 1538 play *Kynge Johan* "calking" is mentioned along with conjuring, coining and other frauds. Nevertheless, it has also been connected to the French noun *cauchemar*, a nightmare. Overall, though, 'calcar' seems to be more to do with sorcery and magic than with Faery.[17]

CHITTIFACES

Skeat's *Glossary of Tudor and Stuart Words* and Wright's *Dialect Dictionary* both define this as someone with a thin and pinched face, a freckled visage or a small baby face. It also is defined as a *puellulus improbulus* – a bad little girl. It might be used contemptuously. Thomas Otway's 1683 play, *The Souldiers Fortune*, includes the line "Now, now, you little Witch, now you Chitsface."[18]

Possibly related is Chaucer's term 'chichevache' which is used in the 'Clerk's Tale' in the *Canterbury Tales* – "Lest Chichevache yow swelwe in hire entraille!" [swallow in her insides]. John

---

16 Francis Osborne, *Advice to a Son*, 1656, 36; King, 'Elegies,' *Poems* (1657).
17 John Bale, *Kynge Johan*, 1538, 1838 edition, 71.
18 T. Otway, *The Souldiers Fortune*, 1683, Act 3, scene 1.

Lydgate's early fifteenth century poem *Bycorne & Chychevache* reaffirms that "Chichevache eteþe wymmen goode." This a monster that devours obedient wives (and therefore is very hungry, according to Chaucer's joke). This creature is contrasted satirically by Lydgate with the *bicorn,* part panther and part cow, which eats devoted husbands and is, apparently, very well fed and plump. Denham mentions *bygorns* in his list as well.[19]

We might also note that in French *chevaucher* means simply 'to ride a horse,' so that a connotation of nightmare may have been incorporated into this name.

CLABBERNAPPERS

Some topographical and historical research reveals that in Southfleet parish in Kent there once was a large cave known that was called the Clabber Napper's Hole. The related legend, as transcribed in the *Gentleman's Magazine* for 1803 and reprinted in vol.26 for December 1846, was that the occupier of the cave was a kidnapper or freebooter. The article proposed that clabber derived from "caer l'abre," the dwelling in the woods, though there is no attempt to explain why a Welsh word and a French word would be combined – as is frequent in old and dodgy etymologies where words with suitable meanings are randomly put together with no thought for historical likelihood.

A more literal interpretation of the name might suggest that it was simply an onomatopoeic word, the meaning of which was a sort of noisy abductor (of children). The Clabber Napper might, therefore, have been a sort of nursery sprite similar to Clap-cans that was used to scare children. If so, it might have been adopted by the putative smugglers to keep people away from their lair, or it might have been used by parents to discourage their children from playing there.

---

19 Chaucer, *Canterbury Tales*, line 1188.

GRINGES

In old dialects, to gringe or grange means to grind the teeth. We may therefore imagine a monster that grinds its teeth a lot – perhaps, like Tom-Dockin, to scare naughty children.[20]

MIFFIES

Miffy is a nickname for the devil in Gloucestershire according to Thomas Wright's *Dictionary of Obsolete and Provincial English*. Presumably it is related to Old French *maufé* meaning the devil. In addition, 'miff' means displeasure or ill humour, hence the modern meaning of being or feeling miffed over something.[21]

MOCK-BEGGARS

There are numerous places known as Mockbeggar, Mock Beggar, or some variant thereon. E. Cobham Brewer's *Dictionary of Phrase and Fable*, 1894, defines Mock-Beggar Hall as an ostentatious dwelling whose owners will turn away the poor from their door.

This is the literal interpretation of the phrase; however, John Florio's 1611 dictionary of English and Italian, *Queen Anna's New World of Words*, also defines 'beffana' (mockbeggar) as a bugbear or scarecrow.

NICKIES & NACKS

The nickies and nacks of Denham's list are water sprites – he also mentioned the related *nixies* (but this is just an adaptation of the German name *nixe* and first seems to have been used in Britain about 1816 by Sir Walter Scott) and *nisses,* which might be

---

20 Dickinson, *Glossary of Words and Phrases Pertaining to the Dialect of Cumberland,* 1878.

21 T. Wright, *Dictionary of Obsolete and Provincial English,* 1857, vol.2.

another pronunciation of the word, but is much more likely to be taken from Swedish and Danish, a *nisse* being a sort of domestic goblin or brownie. Keightley seems to have been one of the first to use it in print in the *Fairy Mythology* (1828), so it is again a late borrowing and not an authentic British sprite; the nisse's role had already been long filled by our own brownies and hobs.

Denham quotes a verse from Keightley's *Fairy Mythology*:

> "Know you the nixies, gay and fair?
> Their eyes are black, and green their hair,
> They lurk in sedgy waters."

Nicks, necks and nickies all can be traced back to Anglo-Saxon word *nicer* or *nicor*, which became *nekir* and *nyker* in Middle English. All the Germanic languages of the continent have related words with a similar meaning. The nickie, neck or nack is a supernatural being found living in the sea or in inland waters – other familiar terms might be water-demon or kelpie. In Middle English the word was also used to denote a siren or mermaid.

The creature first appeared in the poem *Beowulf* as a dreadful creature of the night; it continued to be deadly and terrible in subsequent centuries. In Layamon's historical poem the *Brut,* of about 1200, we are told about a lake in Scotland "Þat water is unimete brade; nikeres þer baðieð inne; þer is æluene ploȝe in atteliche pole" (The water is immeasurably broad; nikers bathe there; elves also play in the same hideous pool).[22]

The confessional treatise *Ayenbite of Inwite* (The Prick of Conscience) of about 1340 describes to us the how sea creatures called "nykeren ... habbeþ bodyes of wyfman and tayl of uisse" (bodies of women and tails of fish). In other words, they can be a sort of mermaid. Like sirens, according to Robert Mannyng in 1338, the nikers will sing a "mery song þat drecched þam ferly long [tormented them for a long time]." The *Treatise of Ghostly*

---

22 Layamon, *Brut,* lines 10851–2.

Battle (1500) also describes their tricks to tempt and lure men: "The nykare or meremaydene, that cast opone the water syde dyverse thyngis whyche semene fayre.to mane, but anone as he taketh hit, she taketh hyme ande devoureth hym." This image persisted into Victorian times: in 1853 in *Hypatia* Charles Kingsley had a character ask "'What is a nicor, Agilmund?' 'A sea-devil who eats sailors.'"[23]

A secondary meaning (but one that is now the common understanding of the word), is demon or devil. So, in 1481, William Caxton's translation of the *History of Reynard Fox* contains a reference to "fowle nyckers, Come they out of helle?" This meaning was preserved in the poem, 'Nickar the Soulless,' published by Sebastian Evans in *Macmillan's Magazine* for 1863 (and later in *Brother Fabian's Manuscript and Other Poems*, 1865). Nickar, the devil, makes a deal for a man's soul so that he may regain his sight and marry the naked faery girl he once saw bathing in a river. Today, of course, we still refer to 'Old Nick.'[24]

At Kebeg, on the Isle of Man, there is a pool on the Ballacoan stream known to be a haunt of a *nyker*. He once abducted a lovely cow girl by answering her calls for her cattle and then bringing down a mist to conceal his kidnapping. Another *nyker*, in the form of a horse or pony, or sometimes a handsome young man, is known to haunt the pond called Nikkesen's Pool in Lonan Parish on the island. In male form, this *nikkesen* sings a beautiful but mournful song in an unknown tongue, with which he tries to tempt girls into the water with him. If a young woman enters his pool, her body is never found again; instead, on moonlit nights, the *nikkesen* may be seen near the pool dancing in a circle with his victims.

In Hampshire, Somerset and along the Welsh Borders, rivers are haunted by Nicky Nicky Nye, who pulls in unwary children.

---

23 Michael of Northgate (trans), *Ayenbite of Inwite*, line 61.
24 Scott, 'The Devil & His Imps,' *Transactions of the American Philological Association*, 119.

In Sussex, there are at least five so-called 'knucker' or 'nucker' holes,' deep, round pools that are reportedly bottomless, in which 'knuckers' live. These monsters are described as winged water serpents; they prey upon livestock and people and can be very hard to kill.[25]

Lastly, in County Durham, a 'black ghost' is seen in Nicky-Nacky Field whilst the goblin of Nicky-Nacky Bridge is blamed for the disappearance of a man one night. The name strongly suggests we are dealing with a water sprite, regardless of the labels that have been applied to the being. There is a Nicker Wood, near Sheffield, which may have been named after a local water sprite according to Sidney Addy. In Yorkshire more widely, Nicky or Nicker-bore is a foolish person drowned after he sat on the wrong end of a branch overhanging a river and sawed it through.[26]

SPOORNS & SPURNS

'Spurn' generally denoted a fight or a spur but in the Dorset dialect it meant an evil spirit. In 1627, playwright Thomas Middleton composed his own short list of awful supernaturals, comprising "Dwarffes, Imps, the Spoorne, the Mare, the Man i' th Oake."[27]

Keightley speculated that both "Calcar and Sporn (spurs?) may be the same, from the idea of riding" and hence some kind of nightmare, an evil spirit that rode people in their sleep and caused frightening dreams and paralysis.[28]

---

25 J. Simpson, *Folklore of the Welsh Border*, 1976, 77; S. Cooper, *A Sussex Book of Witch Legends*, 2020, 223; Simpson, *Folklore of Sussex*, 2009, 34–38; Westwood & Simpson, *Lore of the Land*, 732.

26 Morrison, *Manx Faery Tales*, 1911, 83; Gill, *Manx Scrapbook*, c.4; Mona Douglas, 18; W. Brockie, *Legends & Superstitions of the County of Durham*, 1886, 55; S. Addy, *Glossary of Words Used in the Neighbourhood of Sheffield*, 1888, 158; Wright, *Rustic Speech & Folklore*, 198.

27 Middleton, The *Witch* (1627), Act 1, scene 2, 299.

28 Keightley, *Fairy Mythology*, note to page 334.

TANTARRABOBS

'Tantara' and 'tantaran' was a noise or distubance (as in a *tantr*um). Tantarabobus, Tantarabobs, or Tankerabogus were variants upon a South Western dialect name for the Devil; it also denoted a noisy playful child. Thus, tantara-bogus was a noisy bogle. The name was used once in Somerset and Devon to get naughty children to behave: "Now, Polly, yü've abin a bad, naughty maid, and ef yü be sich a wicked cheel again, I'll zend vur tankerabogus tü come and cār yü away tü 'is pittee-awl" (Now then, Polly, you've been a naughty girl and, if you're bad again, I'll send for Takkerabogus to come and carry you away to his hole in the ground).[29]

THRUMMY CAPS

According to Fife topographer Henry Farnie, Thrummy-cap was the vindictive ghost of a drowned carpenter who haunted the vicinity of the harbour where he died. James Halliwell-Phillips meanwhile reported that thrummy-caps were faeries from Northumberland and were "Queer looking little old men" who lived in the vaults and cellars of castles. They wear a bonnet, have a red face and empty barrels of drink.[30]

John Burness, the cousin of poet Robert Burns, wrote a dramatic poem entitled *Thrummy Cap, A Legend of the Castle of Fiddes*. In this, the name is applied to a man with a rough cap, "baith large an' stout." Staying at Fiddes Castle, Thrummy meets a ghost who is his spitting image and, undismayed, the pair drink and play football together. It's doubtful whether there was ever a ghost legend at Fiddes until Burness invented it.

---

29 Joseph Wright, *English Dialect Dictionary*; Wright, *Rustic Speech & Folkore*, 198.

30 Farnie, *Fife Coast from Queensferry to Fifeness*, 1860, 112–113; Halliwell, *Dictionary of Archaic & Provincial Words*, 1848; W. Brockie, *Legends & Superstitions of the County of Durham*, 1886, 58.

It's probably not immediately clear how or why this relates to a supernatural being, but 'thrum' means a weaver's ends, the extremity of the warp that can't be woven. It is a piece of material about nine inches in width. Thrum therefore meant a frayed fringe or tuft, so that a thrummy-cap would be a ragged or shaggy looking hat knitted from these off-cuts of coarse woven woollen cloth. One suggestion has been that the name is a euphemism for the devil, alluding to his shaggy hair and horns. Fascinatingly, given this last explanation, we may note that Aberdeenshire witch suspect Ellen Gray in 1597 described to her interrogators how the devil himself had appeared to her "in the scheap of ane agit man, beirdit, with a quhyt gown and a thrummit hatt."[31]

TINTS

As a noun, the word is defined as being an obscure northern term for goblin. Another sense of the word 'tint' is a tiny touch, scrap or taste whilst 'tinte' means lost (coming from a Middle English verb of that meaning, *tine,* to lose). Tinted was therefore 'lost' or 'neglected.'[32]

There is a story in which an Eskdale goblin named Gilpin Horner was heard by two men crying out "Tint, tint, tint," the word in this context apparently meaning 'lost.' They responded to his cry, "What de'il's tint you?" (Who the devil's lost – or even taken – you) and the goblin then appeared to them, "something like a human form, but surprisingly little, distorted in features and misshapen in limbs." The men fled and Horner pursued them and took up residence in the home of one of the pair. This creature was "undoubtedly flesh and blood" as it ate and drank with the family and had a taste for cream. This, it stole this to

---

31 Westwood & Kingshill, *The Lore of Scotland,* 2009, 97 'Methil;' *Spalding Club Miscellany,* 1841, 127.

32 J. Wright, *English Dialect Dictionary.*

eat whenever it could; it was also cruel to the children if they provoked it. One day, though, a voice was heard calling the goblin's name and it leapt up and left for ever.[33]

In another legend, a man tried to taunt the duergars (dwarves) of the Simonside Hills in Northumberland by going out one night calling "Tint! tint!" The duergars at first appeared with little lights near a bog, trying to lure him in – much like a will of the wisp – but the story concludes with an "innumerable multitude" of them with "hideous visages" and club in their hands, surrounding the man. He tried to fight them off with his staff but they had no physical forms and, every time he struck out, he only seemed to multiply the number assailing him, until he collapsed in a faint until morning.[34]

WIRRIKOWS

The Scottish wirry-cowe, worricow, and variations thereon, was a bugbear or goblin; the name might also be used for a scarecrow or for the devil himself. The name probably comes from a combination of the words 'worry' (in the sense of harassment) and 'cowe' or hobgoblin. Denham mentions "kows or cowes" separately in his list; an example is the Hedley Kowe of Hedley near Ebchester, which was a mischievous bogie that could take a variety of forms in order to play tricks on its hapless victims.[35]

Examples of the Scottish word's usage are found in Thomas Donaldson's *Poems, Chiefly in the Scottish Dialect* of 1809: "Where harpie, imp, an' warricoe/ An' goblins dwell" and in Sir Walter Scott's 1816 novel *Black Dwarf* – "They do say there's a sort o' worricows and lang-nebbed things about the land." Another

---

33 George Allan, *Life of Sir Walter Scott, Baronet: With Critical Notices of His Writings*, 1834, 247–248.
34 Charles Tibbits, *Folk-lore and Legends: English*, 1890, 182–183.
35 See my *Beyond Faery*, 2020.

poet, Robert Ferguson, connected the word with the devil and with magic, writing "O' warlocks loupin' round the wirrikow/ O' ghaists that win [abide] in glen and kirk yard drear."[36]

The wirrikow was, apparently, a dreadful thing to meet: James Hogg refers in *The Brownie of Bodsbeck* (1818) to "the waefu' [woeful] wirricowe." In James Lumsden's play, *Doun I' Th' Loudons*, the sprite is described as being "Hump-backit an' bow'd – a wirricow/ And scrimply [barely] fowre feet three!" He had a red face, according to Hogg: "haffats in a lowe" and would make people scream with fear and alarm. For example, she "Scream'd at ilk clough, an' skrech'd at ilka how, As sair as she had seen the wirry-cow."[37]

URCHINS

The principal meaning of this word is hedgehog, as it derives through Middle English from the Old French *herichon,* with the same meaning. It acquired additional implications, though, such as a mischievous person, a deformed individual and a youth or a brat (preserved in our modern 'street urchin'). The word also came to denote a goblin or elf and was very widely employed in this sense – as is shown by Scot's and Denham's usage but also, for example, by writer Thomas Nashe: in *Strange Newes* (1592) he referred to "the Fairies and night Urchins" and in his *Terrors of Night* (1594) he mentioned "An old wive's tale of divells and urchins." Two decades later, in the musician Thomas Ravenscroft's *Briefe Discourse,* of 1614, we find urchins dancing in faery rings in the lyric "By the moone we sport and play; Trip it, little Urchins all, Lightly as the little little bee." Later, in Part Two, we shall see Shakespeare using the word in this faery sense in the *Merry Wives of Windsor*. See as well the playwright's

---

36 Donaldson, *Poetical Works,* 38 'Second Epistle to Davie;' Scot, *Tales of my Landlord,* 1st Series, I, 51; Ferguson, *The Farmer's Ingle.*

37 Lumsden, *Loudons,* 1908, 276; A. Ross, *Helenore,* 1768, 77.

Tempest – "But they'll nor pinch, Fright me with Urchyn-shewes, pitch me i'th mire ..." whilst in *Comus,* Milton too used the word as a substitute for faery: "Helping all urchin blasts, and ill lucke signes/ That the shrewd medling elfe delights to make ...".[38]

The word also acquired closely related meanings, such as 'the offspring of the devil:' Samuel Harsnett's *Sermon on Ezekiel* (1583) refers to a "childe of Darkness ... the Urchin of Hel" and in John Beaumont's *Psyche* there's mention of "an Urcheon of Damnation!" The word could also denote a hag.[39]

The *Oxford English Dictionary* proposes that the word 'urchin' was applied to faeries because they could take on that animal's form. Witches were known to do this to steal cow's milk from their udders, but I can't think of a case of faeries looking like hedgehogs. A better explanation might be found in Joseph Ritson's *Dissertation of Fairies.* He recalled that a female relative had described the hobgoblin Lob resting after his labours and "lying before the fire like a great rough hurgin bear." The word 'hurgin' almost definitely should be pronounced with a soft 'g,' indicating that it is a dialect version of 'urchin,' thereby indicating the spiky and unkempt nature of Lob's fur. Equally, the fact that the word carried with it the sense of a mischievous or roguish younger person might have been reason enough to apply it to faeries, who are known for their tricks and mercurial tempers.[40]

---

38 Shakespeare *Tempest* (1623) Act 2, scene 2; Milton, *Comus*, 1637, 29.

39 Harsnett, *Sermon*, published 1658, 129; Beaumont, *Psyche*, 1648, x, xxix, 158; for 'hag' see G. Thornley, *Daphnis & Chloe*, 1657, 203.

40 Ritson, *Dissertation*, 1831, 22–23.

Conclusion

Denham's list is a disorganised heap of names but, as can be seen, with a little effort it can be organised to reveal the richness of British faerylore and the many and varied categories of faery being that have been recognised over the centuries, with their different habitats and habits. Although confirmation probably wasn't wanting, all of this only goes to underline how complex British Faery is. One of the Manx witnesses interviewed by Evans Wentz, John Davies of Ballasalla, told him that "There are as many kinds of fairies as populations in our world." Even when it has been edited and ordered, Denham's list demonstrates how right Davies was.[1]

What is most significant from the preceding discussion is how loosely defined many of the words examined were. Earlier generations either weren't very sure whether a supernatural being was a faery or a demon (which is not impossible) or the boundaries between the terms were rather porous or fluid. Where exactly we draw the line between devil, elf, bogie, hag, phantom or ghost often proves hard to determine. It's important to recognise this, as we'll see, again and again in later chapters, that hard and fast distinctions didn't tend to be made.

---

1 Evans Wentz, *Fairy Faith,* 123.

PART TWO

Faeries & Dreams

Introduction

Faeryland has something of the dreamlike or illusory about it and literary authors often play upon this idea, as – for example – did John Dryden:

> "Methinks we walk in Dreams, on fairyland,
> Where golden Ore lyes mixt with common sand."[1]

The faeries govern dreams, as we shall examine in detail, but their realm is also one which, for humans, is regularly described as resembling a trance-like state:

> "Either we sleep, or dream extravagantly,
> Or else the fairies govern in this house."[2]

Often, those who are 'taken' by the faeries, by means of entrapment in a dance within a faery ring, will return and report that the time spent away was like dreaming. Alternatively, those whose spirits have been abducted, but whose bodies have remained on earth, may be described by friends and family as being in a comatose state akin to a deep dream. The distortions of time and the transformations of matter that are a commonplace aspect of contact with Faery all further contribute to its dream-like quality. As an illustration, a Cornish farmer called Charles Hutchen, of Trevescan (near Sennen at Land's End), described to faery researcher Walter Evans Wentz how once, at St. Just, on Christmas Day, a pisky had twice carried a boy away in his cloak, but the boy had managed to escape from both kidnappings and to return home. Each time the boy was away for only an hour – "probably in a dream or trance state" Evans Wentz added.[3]

---

1   John Dryden, *The Indian Emperor,* 1664, Act I, scene 1.
2   Samuel Tuke, *The Adventures of Five Hours,* 1662, Act V.
3   Evans Wentz, *The Fairy Faith in Celtic Countries,* 1911, 181; identical associations with dreaming are found in Ireland- see pages 41, 50 & 69.

Encounters with the faeries can appear to take place somewhere on the borders of sleep, as an incident from the early seventeenth century in West Wales demonstrates. A man was asleep in bed one night when he awoke to find that over a dozen faery men, women and children had assembled in his bedroom to feast and dance. They remained for four hours, during which time the man was unable to awaken his wife beside him to share in the vision. Eventually the faeries departed, but when the man tried to follow them, he was incapable of finding the door out of the room – or even the way back to his bed – until panic made him cry out, at which point the whole family awoke and the spell dissipated.[4]

Highly comparable are several incidents from the Isle of Man. A woman living at Glenchass was lying in bed after the birth of a baby with a light burning in the room. Her husband was beside her, fast asleep, when she saw a number of faeries peeping in at the door. They soon entered the room and began to make an image. She couldn't tell whether it was meant to be herself or the baby but she was sure they intended to take one or other of them. She tried repeatedly to wake her husband up but he was very soundly asleep and would not stir. Fortunately, before the form the faeries were making was quite finished, she got him roused, and as soon as they heard his voice they fled, dragging the image after them.[5]

The Manx folklorist Charles Roeder was told about two other very similar cases. The first concerned a woman in bed after her confinement, whose husband was ill and was asleep beside her. She heard a voice that seemed to come from the window, calling her name. She replied and, instantly, a man stood beside her. He tried to pick her up, declaring 'Your flesh is mine and your blood is mine.' The woman was unable to waken her husband and, in a panic, blessed herself. The faery man disappeared and, as soon as

---

4 Ceredig Davies, *Folklore*, 123; Baxter, *The Certainty of the World of Spirits*, 130.
5 *Manx Notes & Queries*, 1904, no.126.

he was gone, the husband woke up. Another witness told Roeder about a woman from Barrule who was alone in bed, sick, and was visited there by 'the bishop of the faeries,' who shared a cake with her.[6]

In a Welsh example, a man asleep in his bed at Bwlch y ddar near Llangedwyn awoke to find a small fiddler playing and a group of the *tylwyth teg* dancing in his bedroom. He asked who they were and they told him, *'yspridion yr awyr'* (spirits of the air). This response seems to make it clear that we are witnessing a contact between different dimensions or 'planes' of existence. Some have sought to describe such faery experiences as arising from 'sleep paralysis,' and these particular examples would certainly seem to support that theory. Nonetheless, I think there is more magic and deception involved in this than physiology.[7]

In 1910, Evans Wentz interviewed the Reverend John David Davis, rector of the parishes of Llanmadoc and Cheriton on the Gower peninsula in Wales; he recounted a story concerning the tenant of Eynonsford Farm in Gower. The man "had a dream one night, and in it thought he heard soft sweet music and the patter of dancing feet. Waking up, he beheld his cow-shed, which opened off his bedroom, filled with a multitude of little beings, about one foot high, swarming all over his fat ox, and they were preparing to slaughter the ox. He was so surprised that he could not move. In a short time, the *Verry Volk* had killed, dressed, and eaten the animal. The feast being over, they collected the hide and bones, except one very small leg-bone which they could not find, placed them in position, then stretched the hide over them; and, as the farmer looked, the ox appeared as sound and fat as ever but, when he let it out to pasture in the morning, he observed that it had a slight lameness in the leg lacking the missing bone." The story bears some close resemblances to the previous one from Ceredigion (such as the witness' inability to move), save

---

6 C. Roeder, *Manx Folk-Tales,* 1913, no.31 & 32.
7 *Bye-Gones,* January 4th 1899, 1.

that in this second case the farmer believed he was dreaming – a theory challenged, of course, by the fact of the lameness of the beast the next day.[8]

Evans Wentz ascribed a Breton story of a faery encounter to a possible dream- or trance-like state. He interviewed a woman called Louise Le Rouzic, living at Kerallan, near Carnac, who described to him an incident from her grandfather's lifetime. "There was a young girl who went to the sabbath of the *corrigans* [faeries] and, when she returned and was asked where she had been, said, 'I have travelled over water, wood, and hedges' – and she related all she had seen and heard. Then one night, afterwards, the *corrigans* came into the house, beat her, and dragged her from bed. Upon hearing the uproar, my grandfather arose and found the girl lying flat on the stone floor. 'Never question me again," she said to him, "or they will kill me.'" This story discloses the usual faery anger over having their secrets divulged, but the author's suggestion that the girl's fall from her bed was due to some kind of somnambulism or related state may be doubted given other incidents in which individuals have been abducted or contacted by faeries whilst asleep (see later).

The Irish poet W.B. Yeats expressed the relationship between faeries and dreams in very elegant terms:

> "Many poets, and all mystic and occult writers, in all ages and countries, have declared that behind the visible are chains on chains of conscious beings, who are not of heaven but of the earth, who have no inherent form, but change according to their whim, or the mind that sees them. You cannot lift your hand without influencing and being influenced by hordes. The visible world is merely their skin. In dreams we go amongst them, and play with them, and combat with them. They are, perhaps, human souls in the crucible – these creatures of whim."

---

8 Evans Wentz, *The Fairy Faith in Celtic Countries*, 159.

Evans Wentz concluded his study of the faery faith by declaring that "Fairyland exists as a supernormal state of consciousness into which men and women may enter temporarily in dreams, trances, or in various ecstatic conditions; or for an indefinite period at death."[9]

These comparisons with a liminal waking or sleeping state arise from the difficulties humans appear to experience in formulating in familiar terms what the experience of being in Faery is like. If we think of it as another dimension, mundane terminology is very likely to prove inadequate. This is an almost inevitable consequence arising from the existential gulf between mortals and faeries. What I'm mainly interested in considering here, though, is the manner on which faeries use human dreams to communicate with and interact with us.

---

9 W.B. Yeats, *Irish Fairy and Folk-Tales* (1888), 2; Evans Wentz, *Fairy Faith,* 490.

Sweet Dreams, Wet Dreams & Nightmares

Faery is a highly sexual place and, as a result, it may come as little surprise to learn that many of the manifestations of faeries in and through human dreams occur in an erotic context.

QUEEN MAB

Queen Mab is the archetype of the sensual, sexual faery. She is a passionate individual, closely linked with passion and love. It was widely believed that Mab would fall for young men and choose them as her lovers.[1]

Mab also had a role as the midwife of dreams. Famously, in Shakespeare's *Romeo and Juliet,* Mercutio pictures her enabling sleeping humans to realise their desires for gain in nocturnal fantasy. He describes the queen's appearance and then sets out her role memorably and at some length:

> "She is the fairies' midwife, and she comes
> In shape no bigger than an agate stone
> On the forefinger of an alderman,
> Drawn with a team of little atomi
> Over men's noses as they lie asleep.
> Her wagon spokes made of long spinners' legs,
> The cover of the wings of grasshoppers,
> Her traces of the smallest spider's web,
> Her collars of the moonshine's watery beams,
> Her whip of cricket's bone, the lash of film,
> Her wagoner a small gray-coated gnat,

---

1 *The Cozenages of the Wests,* 1613.

Not half so big as a round little worm
Pricked from the lazy finger of a maid.
Her chariot is an empty hazelnut
Made by the joiner squirrel or old grub,
Time out o' mind the fairies' coachmakers.
And in this state she gallops night by night
Through lovers' brains, and then they dream of love;
On courtiers' knees, that dream on curtsies straight;
O'er lawyers' fingers, who straight dream on fees;
O'er ladies' lips, who straight on kisses dream,
Which oft the angry Mab with blisters plagues,
Because their breaths with sweetmeats tainted are.
Sometime she gallops o'er a courtier's nose,
And then dreams he of smelling out a suit.
And sometime comes she with a tithe-pig's tail
Tickling a parson's nose as he lies asleep,
Then he dreams of another benefice.
Sometime she driveth o'er a soldier's neck,
And then dreams he of cutting foreign throats,
Of breaches, ambuscadoes, Spanish blades,
Of healths five fathom deep, and then anon
Drums in his ear, at which he starts and wakes,
And being thus frighted swears a prayer or two
And sleeps again ..."[2]

Playwright Thomas Randolph also made reference to Mab's connection with dreams of career success. In his play *Hey for Honesty, Down with Knavery,* published in 1651, Dicaeus, a priest, recalls a recent dream which seems to have been fulfilled:

"Last night I laughed in my sleep. The queen of fairy tickled my nose with a tithe-pig's tail. I dreamt of another benefice and see how it comes about!"[3]

---

2 Act One, scene 4.
3 Randolph, *A Pleasant Comedie, entituled Hey for Honesty, Down with Knavery,* translated out of Aristophanes his Plutus, Act II, scene 6.

Mab's interference in human affairs was taken one stage further by Shakespeare though. Not only does she influence humans' earthly careers and material success, she brings lovers dreams of love requited and can even let them experience love consummated too. Romeo's companion explains that:

> "This is the hag, when maids lie on their backs,
> that presses them and learns them first to bear,
> making them women of good carriage."

This part of Mercutio's description explicitly links Mab, the midwife of dreams, to Mab, the sensual, sexual faery queen.

Shakespeare was quite shamelessly plagiarised by Thomas Otway (1652–85) in his play *The History and Fall of Caius Marius*, which was first performed in 1679. The character Sulpitius observes of another that:

> "Oh! The small Queen of Fairies,
> Is busie in his brains; the Mab that comes
> Drawn by a little Team of smallest Atoms
> Over men's noses as they lie asleep.
> In a chariot of an empty Hazel shell,
> Made by a Joyner-Squirrel: in which State
> She gallops Night by Night through Lovers Brains
> And then how wickedly they dream, all know."[4]

In Michael Drayton's faery epic, *Nymphidia*, the sensual nature of these 'wicked' dreams is addressed more explicitly:

> "And Mab, his merry queen, by night,
> Bestrides young folk that lie up-right,
> (in older times the mare that hight.)"

---

4 Otway, *History & Fall,* Act 1, 1.

We shall turn now to examine this sexual aspect of faery dreams in detail.

MEDIEVAL INCUBI AND SUCCUBI

St Augustine, one of the best-known fathers of the early Christian church, had this to say about disturbed sleep and aroused dreams:

> "There is, too, a very general rumour, which many have verified by their own experience, or which trustworthy persons who have heard the experience of others corroborate, that sylvans and fauns, who are commonly called 'incubi,' had often made wicked assaults upon women, and satisfied their lust upon them; and that certain devils, called *Duses* by the Gauls, are constantly attempting and effecting this impurity is so generally affirmed, that it would be impudent to deny it. From these assertions, indeed, I dare not determine whether there be some spirits embodied in an aerial substance (for this element, even when agitated by a fan, is sensibly felt by the body), and who are capable of lust and of mingling sensibly with women ..."[5]

Much medieval literature makes reference to *incubi* and *succubi*, male and female spirits or demons who take on human form to lie with women and men at night. These beings have ancient roots, both classical and Middle Eastern, and are clearly not identical (or even closely related) to our own faery lovers. This notwithstanding, the terminology has come to be used indiscriminately (as with nymphs and satyrs) to describe faery phenomena, so that there has arisen a good deal of confusion or overlap between the two types of spiritual being. So, for example, in Ben Jonson's play *The Sad Shepherd* a character declares "I'm na' Fay! Na' Incubus! Na' Changelin'!"[6]

5 Augustine of Hippo, *Civitas Dei (The City of God)*, Book 15, chapter 23.
6 Jonson, *The Sad Shepherd or a Tale of Robin Hood*, 1637, II, 2.

The incubus as demon and the incubus as faery have existed side by side for many centuries, the church striving to assert the former meaning (for example, even going so far as to argue that devils took on the form of elves in order to seduce people!), yet with the second interpretation persisting, or even gaining precedence, well into the early modern period.[7]

The idea of dangerous incubi and succubi molesting the British population seems to date back (at least) to Anglo-Saxon times. The famous historian, the monk Bede, referred to the problem in the early decades of the eighth century. He was obviously aware of the words of St Augustine, cited above, when he described how demons "can appear as men in female form, or as women in male dress, which the Gauls call *Dusi*; by an unspeakable miracle incorporeal spirits contrive to seek and desire to sleep with a human body." Bede claimed that they would even enter into pacts of love with their mortal partners.[8]

Bede was clear that he was describing demons, but in the work of subsequent writers and chroniclers the exact difference between demons and faeries becomes less and less certain. The writer Walter Map, who died in 1210, composed *De Nugis Curialum,* a collection of anecdotes and stories that includes the tale of Edric the Wild, a man who captured a faery wife for himself. Map referred to this woman as both a faery (*fatalitas*) and a succubus. Also from the late twelfth century comes a story contained in the life of Hugh of Lincoln, which was written by the monk Adam of Eynsham. Adam described how a 'demon' in the shape of a young man pestered a woman for sex. She was advised to get rid of this incubus by picking a herb, which she had to wear in her bosom and scatter around her house. The plant in question was St John's Wort, a herb well-known for repelling faeries, and we shall have cause to mention it and its properties again shortly.

---

7 *Lucydarye*, 55.
8 Bede. *Exposition of Luke's Gospel,* PL92.438B.

The English canon lawyer, Gervase of Tilbury, between 1210 and 1214 composed the *Otia Imperialia*, a text that is a valuable source of early English folklore. He too described *incubi*, stating that they were "demons [who] love women with such a passion that they break out into unheard-of acts of lewdness and, when they come to bed with them, they bear down upon them with extraordinary pressure, and yet are seen by no-one else." Gervase may have followed Augustine and described the incubi as 'demons,' but elsewhere in his book he recognised that these lover spirits were popularly called faeries.[9]

In Robert of Gloucester's *Metrical Chronicle* (composed between about 1260 and 1300) there is an account of the circumstances that surrounded the conception of the famous wizard Merlin. His mother described how an unknown but very handsome man used to come to see her in her room at night and, in due course, she found herself pregnant – never having slept with any other man. Amazed by this story, the king sought his counsellors' advice, and they confirmed that there were 'wights' called elves (both male and female) who were known to act like this and to visit men and women at night.

> *"Þe clerkes sede þat it is in philosofie yfounde*
> *Þat þer beþ in þe eyr an hey fer fram þe grounde*
> *As a maner gostes wiȝtes as it be*
> *Ond me may ȝem ofte an erþe in wilde studes yse*
> *Ond ofte in mannes forme wommen hii comeþ to*
> *Ond ofte in wimmen forme hii comeþ to men al so*
> *Þat men clupeþ eluene ond paraventure in þis manere*
> *On of hom in þis womman biȝet þis child here."*

"The clerks said [to the king] that it's accepted by science
That there are, high in the air and far above the ground,

---

9 Gervase of Tilbury, *Otia Imperialia*, 2002 edition, 96–97 & 730; in fact, Augustine may have recognised the same thing too, when he referred to the 'demons' as sylvans, fauns and dusii.

Beings that resemble ghosts
(Whom you can often see in wild, wooded places
And who often come in the shape of men to women
And who in women's form visit men too)
That we call elves. Perhaps in this way
One of them got this woman here pregnant with this child
[Merlin]."[10]

Robert of Gloucester was, almost certainly, a learned monk, but despite his background and education he was clear that incubi and succubi were elves (or perhaps ghosts) rather than demons, presumably reflecting popular views on the matter. Significantly, from the previous century there's a story of a handsome faery male who seduced a young woman at Dunwich.[11]

Writing about half a century later, in 1350, the Benedictine monk and chronicler, Ranulph Higden (1280–1364), in his book *Speculum Curatorum,* 'The Mirror for Curates,' provided another early English discussion of incubi.[12] Higden's demonic sprites come to sleeping people at night and afflict them with the 'hot ague.' The sleepers feel their hearts being compressed as they lie on their backs and fear that the life within them is being squeezed out. Today we would call this sensation a nightmare; in earlier times it was believed to be a physical, often sexual, assault by a nocturnal demon or faery. Significantly, perhaps, all the other activities that Higden ascribed to his demonic sprites are ones still associated with faery-kind: dancing in circles, disturbing horses at night and dealing in false money.[13]

The religious text titled *Dives and Pauper,* which dates to about 1405, suggests that the conceptions of elves set out by Robert of

---

10 On the supernatural parentage of Merlin see R.F. Green, *Elf Queens & Holy Friars,* 2016, 85–92.

11 *Life of William of Norwich,* by Thomas of Monmouth.

12 Crook & Jennings, *Ranulph Higden: Speculum Curatorum, A Mirror for Curates,* Book I, 2012.

13 *Speculum,* chapter II, 129–131.

Gloucester and Higden did indeed reflect a wider popular belief. We are told how 'the fiend' (the devil):

> "may transfigure hym into lykenesse of man or woman by sufferaunce of god, for mannys synne and womans. And the fendes that tempt folk to lecherie be moste besy to appere in mannys likenes & womans to do lecherie with folk and so bringe them to lecherye. And, in speche of folke [i.e. in English], they be cleped [called] elvys, but in Latyne, whan they appeir in mannis lykenes, they be cleped *incubi*. And whane they appier in lykenesse of wymen: they be cleped *succubi*..."

Lastly, John Lydgate composed his poem, *Troy Book,* very early in the fifteenth century. Interestingly, like Gervase of Tilbury before him, he traced incubi back to St Augustine and gave them a classical gloss, referring to: "diverse goddis of þe wodis greene, [that] appere þere, called Satiry, Bycornys, eke, fawny and incubi ...". In the mid-fourteenth century story of Saint Marina, found in the Vernon manuscript, another sylvan creature performs in a similar way: "[a] wodewose wilde/ who gat on hire þis forseyde childe." The *wodewose* is the English wild man of the woods, closely comparable to satyrs and fauns, and also – according to this text – identical to incubi. From these last examples, it will be apparent that all meaningful distinction or separation between fiends, faeries, fauns, demons, incubi and succubi seems to have been lost by this point. They are treated as one and the same species of supernatural entity, but with the faery interpretation steadily gaining precedence.[14]

EARLY MODERN FAERY LOVERS

The idea of faery men appearing in women's beds and coupling with them in fact proved to be a very long lasting one. Puck,

---

14 *Dives et Pauper,* c.21; Bodleian Library MS. Eng. poet. a. 1, lines 209–210.

or Robin Goodfellow, was the offspring of just such a union, according to the story of his *Mad Pranks and Merry Jests,* published in 1628. His father Oberon visited a "proper young Wench" in her bedroom at night, first dancing with her, giving her silver and jewels, and then seducing her. Interestingly, an early sixteenth century conjurer called William Stapleton referred to two spirits he dealt with by the names of Oberon and Inchubus, suggesting an equation between the two.[15]

Reginald Scot included *incubus* amongst his list of demons in the *Discoverie of Witchcraft* of 1584, primarily discussing them in the context of witches and their claimed copulation together. He stated that, until 1400, the devil in the form of a bawdy incubus would have intercourse with women against their wills, but that since then witches had willingly consented to such lechery – and over extended periods. Scot regarded all such claims as being the combined result of falsehood and the misunderstanding of a natural illness. There follows a chapter titled "Of vain Apparitions: how people have been brought to fear Bugs" which seeks expose how many people are kept in fear by a litany of imaginary monsters:

> "But certainly, some one knave in a white sheet hath cosened and abused many thousands ... specially when *Robin Good-fellow* kept such a coil in the Countrey. But you shall understand, that these Bugs specially are spyed and feared of [by] sick folk, children, women, and cowards, which through weakness of mind and body, are shaken with vain dreams and continual fear ... But in our childhood, our Mothers' maids have so terrified us with an ugly Devil having horns on his head, fire in his mouth, and a tail in his breech, eyes like a bason, fangs like a Dog, claws like a Bear, a skin like a Niger, and a voyce roaring like a Lyon, whereby

---

15 K. Briggs, *Some Seventeenth Century Books of Magic,'* Folklore, vol.64, 1953, 448.

we start and are afraid when we hear one cry 'Bough:' and they have so frayed us with Bul-beggers, Spirits, Witches, Urchens, Elves, Hags, Fairies, Satyrs, Pans, Faunes, Sylens [sylvans], Kit with the canstick, Tritons, Centaures, Dwarfes, Gyants, Imps, Calcars, Conjurers, Nymphes, Changelings, *Incubus,* Robin Goodfellow, the Spoorn, the Mare, the man in the Oak, the Hell-wain, the firedrake, the Puckle, Tom-thombe, Hob-goblin, Tom-tumbler, Boneless, and such other Bugs, that we are afraid of our own shadows: insomuch that some never fear the Devil, but in a dark night; and then a polled Sheep is a perilous beast, and many times is taken for our Father's soul, specially in a Churchyard, where a right hardy man heretofore scant durst passe by night, but his hair would stand upright."

For Scot, the incubus ranked with all types of faeries as "vain dreams." Plainly, too, he was highly sceptical about every form of supernatural phenomenon that caused people to suffer baseless alarms. It is just as clear from the 'Shepherd's Dream' in William Warner's *Albion's England* (1612) that the poet was a rationalist and sceptic like Scot and was inclined to suspect that the incubus, "that begets dadlesse babes on girles asleepe" was really just a cover for a much simpler explanation for pregnancies out of marriage.[16]

In the *Discourse Concerning the Nature and Substance of Devils and Spirits,* that was added to the third edition of Scot's book in 1665, there is further discussion of incubi. In particular, a general chapter on 'astral spirits' considers the relationship of incubi to faeries. It stated that "Besides the innumerable Troops of Terrestrial Spirits called Nymphes ... Another sort are the *Incubi,* and *Succubi* ... To these *Incubi* are attributed the diseases of the blood called the *Night-hag,* which certainly have a natural cause,

16 Scot, *Discoverie,* Book 7 c.15 and the 'Discourse' c.11; Denham expanded on this list.

although at the instant of time when the party is oppressed, it is probable that certain malevolent Spirits may mix themselves therein and terrifie the soul and minde of the afflicted party." The writer also cited an unlikely rabbinical authority to the effect "That God made the Fairies, Bugs, Incubus, Robin Good-fellow, and other familiar or domestical Spirits and Devils …".[17]

The faery as incubus-rapist may be best epitomised by an incident from the Orkney island of Stronsay, recorded by the traveller John Ben, perhaps as early as 1529. Here, he was dealing with the activities of trows, which he sketched for his readers:

> "Furthermore sea-monsters called Trowis very often go with the women living there … This is a description of that monster: it is clad in seaweed, in its whole body it is like a foal, with curly hair, it has a member like that of a horse and large testicles."

Ben then reported a case that had occurred whilst he lived on the island:

> "… a beautiful woman, married to an able-bodied farmer, was much tormented by a great spirit, and they were seen, against the husband's will, lying together on one bed. The woman at last became emaciated through sorrow. I advised that she might get freedom by prayer, alms giving, and fasting, which she performed; the duration of her trouble lasted a year."[18]

Two further cases, from the seventeenth century, are very informative about contemporary British beliefs regarding faery lovers. Firstly, there is that of Elspeth Reoch, who was tried and executed for witchcraft at Kirkwall on Orkney in 1616. Elspeth

---

17 Scot, *Discourse*, Book 2, chapter 4, para.14; Book 1, c.11.
18 J. Ben, *Descriptio Insularum Orchadiarum (Description of the Orkney Islands)*, 1529, 'Stronsay.'

confessed to a sexual relationship with a faery man called John Stewart. He had initially approached her when she was twelve, and living at Lochaber, when he had chatted her up, telling her she was "ane prettie." At some point before she was fourteen, Stewart had reappeared, visiting her three nights in a row, pestering her for sex and touching her until she submitted and he "seemed to lie with her." Clearly this faery's behaviour was identical to that of an incubus.[19]

Secondly, there is the remarkable account of Goodwin Wharton (1653–1704) and his dealings with a woman called Mary Parrish, who claimed to have contacts in the faery kingdom of Lowlands, which lies beneath Hounslow Heath, west of London. The story is mainly one of a wealthy man being cheated by a woman who holds out hopes of faery riches and power, but it has a sexual element too.

Parrish told Wharton that the recently widowed faery queen, Queen Penelope LaGard, had taken a fancy to him and wished to marry him and make him the new king of Lowlands. Although plans for face-to-face meetings kept falling through, Wharton had proved so irresistible to Penelope that for some weeks she secretly visited him at night and had sex with him whilst he was asleep. Despite his unconscious state, they had intercourse multiple times nightly, a revelation that for Wharton satisfactorily explained the great tiredness and backache that had recently afflicted him.

Thinking about this fatigue, Wharton realised that he could actually remember one occasion on which he and Queen Penelope had enjoyed sex three times in a row; on the third occasion, the queen had "sucked up her breath" just as they both reached orgasm, the effect of which had been to extract "the very substance of the marrow" from his bones, leaving him drained nearly to the point of death. This statement accords well with

---

19 Black, *Examples of Printed Folklore Concerning Orkney & The Shetland Islands,* 1903, 111.

traditional medical beliefs, that saw sperm as a special kind of 'marrow' or vital energy. Queen Penelope was therefore behaving exactly like a succubus and was sapping Wharton's vital strength.

As with Queen Penelope and the Stronsay trow, the majority of British faery lovers – such as the *leannan sith* of the Scottish Highlands and the Manx *lhiannan shee* – tend to be involved on a longer-term basis with human partners, rather than simply visiting them once for sexual purposes. Writing as late as 1810, Scottish topographer Patrick Grahame observed that "in our Highlands, there be many fair ladies of this aerial order, which do often tryst with amorous youths, in the quality of succubi, or lightsome paramours and strumpets called *lean-nain-sith.*" Still, alongside these enduring love affairs, there is some native evidence for a purely carnal faery visitant, 'the nightmare,' which will be discussed separately in the next section. [20]

Around the same time as the cases just mentioned, Sir Francis Kynaston offered an isolated but interesting explanation of the phenomenon of faery changelings. Instead of regarding them as being elderly faery men who had been substituted for human babies, Kynaston understood them as the offspring of humans and incubi:

> "And many times forsaken our owne kinde,
> Wee are in league with mortals so combinde,
> As that in dreams wee lye with them by night,
> Begetting children, which do Changelings hight."[21]

Kynaston's statement seems unique, but there is just a little more evidence to support it. The Scots term for a changeling is a 'shargie bairn.' A dialect word of northern England is the verb, *sharge,* which is delicately glossed in Halliwell's 1889 *Dictionary*

---

20 P. Grahame, *Sketches Descriptive of Picturesque Scenery in Perthshire,* 1810, 275; for more on the *leannan-sith/ lhiannan-shee,* see my *Love and Sex in Faeryland.*

21 Kynaston, *Leoline & Sydanus,* 1642, stanza 377.

of Dialect and Provincial Words as '*futuo.*' This Latin verb is, in turn, defined by the *Chambers Murray Latin-English Dictionary* as meaning "to have connection with a female." In plain terms, then, 'to sharge' is to have sexual intercourse. Now, it need hardly be remarked that for most of human history children arose solely as the result of sex, so calling a child a "shag baby" wasn't saying very much at all. However, if the phrase implied that the infant might be the result of coupling with an incubus, it may be rather more significant. In fact, in 1645 a woman called Ellen Driver from Framlingham in Suffolk was accused of witchcraft. She claimed, fascinatingly, that she had been married for sixty years to the devil and had borne two children with him, which she called changelings.

FAERIES, SLEEP & DREAMS

It may be worth noting that several Scottish cases in which women were accused of witchcraft also involved their abduction by the faeries from their beds. Isabell Haldane, of Perth, was carried from her bed to a faery hill, where she spent three days and acquired knowledge of the future and of cures. Janet Trall, a friend of Isabell's, was also taken from her child bed, albeit to be "puddled and troubled" by the faery folk in a nearby pool. Bessie Dunlop from Ayrshire was visited by the faery queen herself as she lay in bed after the birth of a child. Perhaps the two latter cases cast new light on the story of the *Fatal Peat Ember* recounted by Evans Wentz. The mother of a newly delivered child lay in bed "gazing dreamily" when she was astonished to see three strange little women enter the room with the intention of stealing the new-born baby from the lap of a nurse dozing by the fire. In the story the faeries are defeated – albeit only temporarily.[22]

---

22 *Extracts from the Presbytery Book of Strathboyce*, x & xi; Pitcairn, *Ancient Criminal Trials*, vol.1, 49–58; Evans Wentz, *Fairy Faith*, 96–97.

Normally, the presence of faery women near a mortal female recently delivered of a child would be treated as evidence of their intention to steal that infant – whether or not an elvish substitute might be left behind in exchange. Sometimes the mother might be taken as well. Nonetheless, the connection of faeries to sleep and the dreaming state that we've been exploring might indicate that there may be other layers of meaning in these reports. Perhaps the faeries' relationship to the women and their offspring was more than merely a matter of kidnapping.

Seductions are very likely to take place at night and in bedrooms for a variety of reasons – secrecy and convenience being the most obvious. Nonetheless, it's notable how in several stories the faery lovers appear beside the human's bed, perhaps indicating that there is an unspoken 'dream-lover' aspect to these cases.

The first instance seems to be a fairly straightforward example of dream communication. A man from Caernarfonshire discovered a mermaid on the seashore. They became friendly and she encouraged his interest by bringing him treasure from under the sea. Then, she visited him as he slept in his bed at night and told him to meet her the next day. When he did, the mermaid was present in human form, wearing a dress, and apparently willing to come on to the land and live with him. Eventually they married and had children together.[23]

In a second example, from the Isle of Man, a man from Derbyhaven called Mickleby was picked up by a *shee* woman at a dance he had stumbled across. He was never able to shake her off afterwards; she would appear beside his bed at night. It was said that he had become tied to her because, after dancing, he had wiped the sweat from his face on part of her dress, thereby creating some physical connection between the pair. Nonetheless, this bond seems to have been most effective at night and, what's more, it could only be severed by throwing an unbleached linen

---

23 J. Rhys, *Celtic Folklore,* vol.1, 117.

sheet over the two of them. This suggests that the 'marital' bed somehow formed a key to their link. Wiping his face had shared a bodily fluid with her (maybe the sweat was a metaphor); covering her with a sheet which had *not* been laid upon during intercourse perhaps counteracted that process.[24]

In an example from Tiree, a herdsman from Baile-phuill fell asleep one warm summer afternoon on the hillock of *Cnoc Ghrianal*. He was rudely woken by a violent slap on his ear. On rubbing his eyes and looking up, he saw a woman in a green dress, the most beautiful female he had ever seen, walking away from him. She headed westward and he followed her for some distance, until she suddenly vanished. This woman was plainly a faery – judging by her dress and by her travel towards the west, known as the faery direction in the Highlands. The slap she gave him could have been punishment for sleeping on the faery hill, but there was clearly more to it than that, even though the story is abruptly curtailed.[25]

Considering the fate of a male from Iona, we might judge the Tiree herdsman to have been lucky. Thinking that it was dawn, the Iona man got up early one morning and went out fishing. After catching some fish, he realised that bright moonlight had fooled him into thinking it was day, so he decided to return home. On the way, he sat down to rest on a hillock and fell asleep. He was awakened by a tugging at the fishing rod, which was still in his hand. The rod was being pulled one way and the fish he'd caught another. Next, he heard the sound of a woman weeping. He suspected she was a faery and tried to get away from her but she caught him and thrashed him soundly. Then, every night after that, he was compelled to meet her and could never again escape her.[26]

---

24 Gill, *Second Manx Scrapbook,* c.6; Evans-Wentz, *Fairy Faith,* 124; *Manx Notes & Queries,* 1904, note 128.

25 J.G. Campbell, *Superstitions of the Highlands & Islands of Scotland,* 1900, 105.

26 Campbell, *Superstitions,* 107.

In these accounts it seems to me that the fact that the victim has fallen asleep is more than just incidental or superfluous detail. Rather, it appears to be a central element in the entrapment by the faery lover. Perhaps sleep is a time when a person is vulnerable, when it is possible for faeries to use dreams to pass into the mortal world and to make contact. One account from the Isle of Man even implies that the faeries can send people to sleep. A woman at Bradda was confined after her child was born and was in her bedroom whilst two other women, who were caring for the baby, sat in the parlour. A candle was lit but, as its flame died down, the two women started to fall asleep. When the women awoke with a jolt, the flame flared up again. Eventually they fell asleep and the candle went out completely. However, they were soon awoken by a disturbance in the bedroom – they lit the candle and found the mother out of bed and heard voices outside complaining that, "[if] only for you, we might have had her." A kidnapping of the mother (or possibly the baby girl) had narrowly been averted.[27]

That humankind was at particular risk during the hours of darkness and sleep was widely understood; the collection of Gaelic prayers and verses known as the *Carmina Gadelica* contain numerous charms invoking the protection of the trinity and the saints overnight. Similar blessings were invoked against faeries (as we'll see in the next section). Closely comparable is a charm explicitly against faeries from the Isle of Man, which calls on St Columb Killey to protect "each window and each door/ And every hole admitting moonlight."[28]

HAGS & NIGHTMARES

Certain Old English medical texts refer to various illnesses that are caused by or related to elves, amongst which is the condition

---

27 Roeder, *Manx Folk-Tales,* no.29.
28 See my *Darker Side of Faery,* 2021, 187–191 & *Mona Miscellany,* 2nd series, vol.21, 1873, 195.

called *aelfsidenn,* a term that literally means 'elf-enchantment' and which seems to be a night fever or nightmares. There is also a charm in the leechbooks against a dwarf or "spider wight" who arrives at night, halter in hand, prepared to ride the victim like a hackney horse over the sea. This link between the faeries, terrifying dreams and the feeling of being ridden appears to be an ancient one – it is also extremely widespread. For example, in Brittany the beings called *corrigans* and *lutins* are said to cause nightmares.[29]

The idea that faery-kind were somehow responsible for, or linked with, nightmares persisted into the early modern period. Samuel Rowlands in 1612 lumped together a wide range of supernatural beings, describing in a play how at night:

> "Great store of Goblins, Faeries, Bugs, Nightmares,
> Urchins and Elves, to many a house repairs."[30]

The same was the case in George Gascoigne's play, *The Buggbears,* which was a translation from Tasso dating to about 1565. He listed in one sentence a range of supernatural beings that must, presumably, be associated:

> "puckes, puckerels, hob howlard, bygorn and Robin Good-fellow … Pickhornes, hob Goblin, Rawhead, bloudiebone the ouglie, Hagges, Buggbears and hellhoundes and Hecate the nightmare."[31]

The common theme in both Rowland's and Gascoigne's lists seems to be the terrifying nature of the entities they mentioned.

---

29 Cockayne, *Leechdoms, Wortcunning, and Starcraft of Early England*, vol.3, 1864, 43, no.56; G, Kittredge, *Witchcraft in Old & New England,* 1929, 218; Evans Wentz, *Fairy Faith,* 207.

30 Samuel Rowlands, *More Knaves Yet?* 1612.

31 H. Dragstra, 'Bull-beggars,' in J. Veenstra, *Airy Nothings – Imagining the Other World of Faerie from the Middle Ages to the Age of Reason,* 2013; Gascoigne, Act III, lines 57 & 70.

The intertwining of faeries and bad dreams was highlighted again in the play *The Ordinary,* by William Cartwright (1611–43), in which Moth prays that:

"St Francis and St Benedict,
Blesse this house from wicked wight,
From the Nightmare and the Goblin,
That is hight Goodfellow Robin..."[32]

As we've already seen in Part One, goblins personified a range of unpleasant characteristics. They were "ill-natured" and frightful and could cause people profound shocks. Like ghosts, they haunted at night and might even invade a sleeper's dreams. It would appear, then, that Cartwright regarded goblins, Robin Goodfellow and nightmares as all essentially identical. Likewise, in their 1621 play *Thierry and Theodoret,* playwrights Beaumont and Fletcher discussed the cause and nature of the unpleasant and exhausting nightmares, with a character complaining that "goblins ride me in my sleep to jelly."[33]

In Scotland, the name 'Mirryland' seems to have been used as another name for Faery – a place more usually referred to as Elphame in Scots. May, Marie, Maiden and Murray-land were variants also used.[34] The name doesn't refer to joy or springtime and certainly doesn't seem to have anything to do with the Virgin Mary, although her presence in people's minds may well have affected the pronunciation. Rather, its root appears to be a great deal older. The name seems to descend from the Anglo-Saxon *maere,* a word that's preserved in the modern English 'nightmare' and which was glossed as 'satyr' in one Old English source (and recall here St Augustine's reference to incubi as a type of

---

32 Cartwright, *The Ordinary*, 1651, Act III, scene 1.
33 Beaumont & Fletcher, Act I, scene 2.
34 See the anonymous verse romance *King Berdok* and Thomas Dunbar's poem *In Secreit Place This Hyndir Nicht;* see too the ballad, 'The rain rins down through Mirry-land toune.'

"sylvans and fauns"). In light of this derivation, 'goblin land' or even 'nightmare land' might be the most reasonable translation of the Scots name. The name again clearly implies some strong connection between sprites, or incubi, and faeries.'[35]

This established – if little known – link between faeries and nightmares is something we've already seen expressed in *Romeo and Juliet*, when Mercutio refers to Queen Mab as "the hag" who presses upon maidens lying in their beds, thereby teaching them "first to bear/ making them women of good carriage." It's pretty evident here that Shakespeare saw Mab as having a sexual function. She educates – and maybe even seduces – virgin girls, teaching them how to perform in bed. The 'bearing', or 'carriage,' to which Mercutio alludes is not about deportment but about receiving a lover lying on top – in the first instance, he allusively suggests, the faery queen riding the maiden for the first time.[36]

In the early modern period, to be 'hag-rid' or 'hag-ridden' was to suffer nightmares, 'the hagge' being conceived to be a hideous witch or succubus who sat on a sleeper's stomach and caused bad dreams. For example, in the *Mad Pranks and Merry Jests of Robin Goodfellow*,[37] Gull the Faery describes how "Many times I get on men and women and so lie on their stomachs that I cause them great pain; for which they call me by the name of Hagge and Nightmare." The victim's experience is that –

> "the nightmare hath prest,
> With that weight on their breast,
> No returnes of their breath can pass."[38]

This notion of compression was a very early one, as we see from the *South English Legendary* of about 1300:

---

35 Spence, *British Fairy Origins*, 46.
36 *Romeo & Juliet* Act I, scene 4.
37 1588, Percy Society, 1841, p.42.
38 *The Holly Bush*, 1646.

"Þe luþere gostes ... deriez men in heore slep ... And ofte huy over-liggez [men], and men cleopiet þe niȝt-mare."

"The evil ghosts harm men in their sleep and often lie on top of them, which people call 'the night-mare.'"

There's obviously a supernatural cause indicated here, albeit not a faery one. However, by the early seventeenth century the fae nature of the affliction had become firmly established. The sixteenth century Scots poem, *My Heart is High Above*, conveys again some sense of how the experience feels: "Then languor on me lies, like Morpheus the mair." In his *Daemonologie* of 1597, King James VI/ I discussed "That abhominable kinde of the Devils abusing of men or women, [which] was called of old, *Incubi* and *Succubi*, according to the difference of the sexes that they conversed with." He explains that these spirits are "the thing which we call the mare, which takes folks sleeping in their beds." At the same timer, James was in no doubt that what were "called vulgarly the Fayrie" were really devils.[39]

The Anglo-Saxon word *mære/mæra* derives from a verb meaning 'to crush.' In modern English it has fallen together with the word for a female horse (Anglo-Saxon *mere*). The words have entirely separate origins, but the sense of riding presumably encouraged the confusion. It seems that this worked in several directions: for instance, in 1696 John Aubrey in his *Miscellanies* described the measures taken in stables to stop faeries taking and riding horses at night:

"To hinder the night mare, they hang in a string, a flint with a hole in it (naturally) by the manger; but best of all they say, hung about their necks, and a flint will do it that hath not a hole in it. It is to prevent the nightmare, viz. the hag, from riding their horses, who will sometimes sweat all night. The flint thus hung does hinder it."

---

39 James Stewart, *Daemonologie,* chapter 3, 67–69 & c.2, 57.

These so-called 'hag-stones' worked as a charm against faery interference. What's particularly notable here is how Aubrey (or rather the country people he spoke to) had understandably, but mistakenly, expanded the term for a faery dream to cover another quite unconnected faery action.[40]

Aubrey wasn't alone confusing different aspects of faery activity. Devon poet, Robert Herrick, in his poem *The Hag*, also described the sensation of a being riding a sleeper like a horse:

> "The Hag is astride,
> This night for to ride;
> The Devill and shee together:"

This isn't merely a bad dream, though, for Herrick went on to depict the victim being bodily abused and very clearly treated like a horse:

> "A Thorn or a Burr
> She takes for a Spurre:
> With a lash of a Bramble she rides now,
> Through Brakes and through Bryars,
> O're Ditches, and Mires ..."

Equally, in *Another Charm for Stables,* Herrick recommended remedies to this hag-riding of actual horses:

> "Hang up hooks and shears to scare
> Hence the hag that rides the mare,
> Till they be all over wet
> With the mire and the sweat:
> This observ'd, the manes shall be
> Of your horses all knot-free."

---

40 Aubrey, *Miscellanies Upon Various Subjects,* under 'Magick.'

So, we see that the metaphorical sense of riding by a supernatural being became inextricably compounded with the idea of actual, physical faery riding of horses (for which, see Part Four). What's more, the sensation of being ridden and pressed on by a faery got mixed up with the idea of sexual riding. In 1548, physician Andrew Borde recommended a herbal remedy for sexual dreams. He explained that the Latin terms incubus and succubus:

> "In Englyshe [are] named the Mare. And some say that it is a kind of spirites, the which doth infect and trouble men when they be in theyr beddes slepynge, as Saint Augustine saythe … I have red … that there is an herbe named *fuga Demonum,* or as the Grecians do name it *Ipericon.* In Englyshe it is named saynt Johns worte, the which herbe is of that virtue that it doth repell suche malyfycyousnes or spirites."[41]

You may recall that we have already seen St John's Wort (*Hypericum perforatum*) being used in the late 1100s to repel sexual assaults by faeries.

Generally, the pressure and shortness of breath of the nightmare were associated with fear rather than sexual activity and arousal, but it's clear there was great confusion between the two aspects of the experience. We see this in William Sampson's 1636 play *The Vow Breaker, or the Fair Maid of Clifton in Nottinghamshire,* when Ursula remarks to Anne:

> "you us'd to say Hobgoblins, Fairies and the like were nothing but our own affrightments and yea, oh my Cuz, I once dreamed of a young batchelor and was ridden with a Nightmare."

Here we elide seamlessly from faeries to nightmares to sexual fantasy within a single sentence. As we read earlier, in Michael

---

41 Borde, *The Fyrst Boke of the Introduction of Knowledge,* 1548, 78–79.

Drayton's verse epic *Nymphidia* the sensual nature of the experience is addressed far more explicitly:

> "And Mab, his merry queen, by night,
> Bestrides young folk that lie up-right,
> (in older times the mare that hight)."

In both of these passages, the poets' bawdiness is barely concealed. Ursula being ridden by her lusty young bachelor and the 'up-right' wet-dreamers of Drayton are almost solely descriptions of erotic fantasy rather than horror. This sexual aspect of the nightmare was underlined by Edward Topsell in his *Historie of Serpents,* where he mentioned "The spirits of the night, called Incubi and Succubi, or else Night-mares."[42]

So, we have come full circle, from the nightmare as a terrifying dream to hag-riding as (lesbian) sex with Queen Mab. This view of the faery queen may well seem like a modern reading of the texts, but such an interpretation is at least two hundred years old. The Swiss-born painter Henry Fuseli (Johann Heinrich Füssli,1741–1825) seems to have been in no doubt about the queen as the bringer of sensual dreams and as a seducer. His picture *Queen Mab,* of 1814, depicts a woman asleep on her couch. Mab is a diminutive figure in the background here, not immediately apparent; she has descended on a shaft of light, accompanied by moths and other faery beings, and she waves her wand over the sleeper. The queen is conjuring the sleeper's dreams, and those are clearly sexual. The slumberer's shift has slipped down to reveal her breasts; to one side, on a dressing table, a tiny, naked female admires herself in the human woman's mirror, attended by another winged fae. We should also note Fuseli's *Fairy Mab* of 1795–96, which shows a wanton, bare breasted monarch.

---

42 Topsell, *Serpents,* 1658, 173.

Even more overtly sexual (and sapphic) is the same artist's *Mab Appears to Two Girls* (roughly dated 1800–20): the young women are naked in bed together, one being asleep whilst her partner admires and caresses her lover's body. Mab is seen descending into their bedroom through parted curtains behind them, once again riding a beam of light. In the corner, a shadowy homunculus sits – perhaps one of those goblins that we have seen are connected with disturbed dreams. Such monstrosities are common in Fuseli's work, as (indeed) are erotic scenes. In this case, Mab's arrival with the pair is unexplained, though perhaps Fuseli wished us to fantasise about a threesome. Alternatively, the apparently sleeping woman, her head turned away from her friend into the crook of her arm, might be experiencing some embarrassment or doubt and Mab, the sexual instructor, could be there to encourage her to surrender herself to her suppressed desires.

Equally significant, perhaps, is Fuseli's *The Incubus Leaving Two Young Women*. This picture might almost be a sequel to the scene just described. A tiny figure on horseback leaps out through the open window. One of the pair on the bed is asleep; her companion is awake, looking in our direction with a tormented expression whilst her hand plays over her bare breasts. Presumably she has been ravished against her will by the incubus.

Lastly, Fuseli's *The Night-Hag Visiting Lapland Witches* (1796) illustrates a passage from Milton's *Paradise Lost* in which the hellhounds surrounding Sin are compared to those who:

> "follow the night-hag when, called
> In secret, riding through the air she comes,
> Lured with the smell of infant blood, to dance
> With Lapland witches, while the labouring moon
> Eclipses at their charms."

In his poem, Milton uses 'night-hag' as an epithet of the Greek goddess Hecate, who presided over witchcraft and magical rites. In the painting, a large breasted witch is preparing a child for sacrifice to Hecate; the infant's naked body is prone on a flat stone before her and a dagger is offered, but she also caresses one thigh in a distinctly sensual manner.[43]

WET DREAMS

Queen Mab clearly used to play a leading role in the seduction of young women – and a few men – during their sleep, but she was not alone in this. In the late seventeenth century, the Reverend Robert Kirk described the local Scottish version of the faery lover – and combined it with the nightmare:

> "For in our Highlands, as there may be many fair Ladies of this aereal Order, which do often tryst with lascivious young Men, in the quality of Succubi, or lightsome Paramours and Strumpets, called Leannain Sith, or familiar Spirits (in Dewter. 18, 11); so, do many of our Hyghlanders, as if a strangling by the Night Mare, pressed with a fearfull Dream, or rather possessed by one of our aereall Neighbours ..."[44]

In the account of his *Mad Pranks and Merry Jests*, Robin Goodfellow mentions how "young wenches sleepe, Till their dreames wake them." This is very likely not just a matter of being awoken by scary dreams; it is probable that erotic fantasies are what disturb them, accompanied by a sensation of weight pressing down.

SWEET DREAMS

As we've seen, Queen Mab was the midwife of dreams and could bring sleepers happy reveries of success in love and business. Yet,

---

43 John Milton, *Paradise Lost,* II, 622–66.
44 Kirk, *Secret Commonwealth,* 'Succint Accompt,' 61.

though she is famed for this, other faeries than Mab seem to be able to bring us sweet dreams.

We have already seen some mention of the link between Robin Goodfellow and (bad) dreams. In the *Life of Robin Goodfellow*, published in 1628, Robin is presented with a linen waistcoat and responds adversely, exclaiming:

> "Because thou lay'st me himpen, hampen,
> I will neither bolt nor stampen.
> 'Tis not your garments new or old,
> That Robin loves; I feele no cold.
> Had you left me milke or creame,
> You should have had a pleasing dreame;
> Because you left no drop nor crum,
> Robin never more will come."

In *Robin Goodfellow, his Mad Pranks* of 1628 there is another reference to his benign influence. One form that Robin can take is that of the bellman, or nightwatchman, who cries "May you dream of your delights/ In your sleeps, see pleasing sights."

For that matter, Robin himself discovers his paternity when he has a dream in which his true parentage is disclosed to him: he receives a scroll that informs him that King Oberon is his father (see earlier) and that he has inherited from him his magical, faery powers.

In the South West of England, there used once to be some association between pixies, moths and happy dreams, the details of which are now largely forgotten. According to writer J. Henry Harris, Cornish mothers used to tell their children that the little brown pisgie moth would play tricks on them in their sleep. In her story of 'The Little Cake Bird' North Cornish author Enys Tregarthen recorded that the belief around St Columb was that the faeries would pass over your nose and arrange your dreams whilst you slept.[45]

---

45 *Cornish Saints and Sinners,* 1907, c.20; Tregarthen, *North Cornwall Fairies & Legends,* 110.

The Devonshire pixies were reported to bring nightmares to some and sweet dreams to others whilst another writer has said that the Cornish pixies will tickle your nose to awaken you when you're having a bad dream. These are rather scattered and inconclusive references, but they underline the existence of a faery link to dreams, even if the full detail of that is now lost to us.[46]

SUMMARY

All in all, it will be clear that there is a complex interaction between many aspects of Faery and humans' sleeping and dreaming. Whether we ascribe this influence to faeries, hags or goblins (or even to ghosts or demons) the evidence indicates that our contact with the supernatural, both physical and psychological, can frequently take place in some strange, trance-like (or entranced) state that exists between waking and sleep-between the human world and another.

So far, we've mainly talked about sex and terror, but the intercourse or communication between faery and mortal can take several forms.

---

46 Bowring, 'Devonshire Pixies,' *Once a Week Magazine,* vol.16, Jan.–June 1867, 206; Harris, *Cornish Saints & Sinners,* c.19.

Communicating through Dreams

It appears that one of the primary means by which faeries communicate with mortals is through the latter's dreams. One of our earliest examples is the late thirteenth or early fourteenth century poem *Sir Orfeo,* in which the faery king meets with Orfeo's wife, Queen Heurodis, whilst she sleeps one May morning under a tree.

In the folklore, communication with mortals through dreams is especially seen in cases where women abducted by the faeries contact their husbands. In a story from Morvern in the west of Scotland, a woman and her baby from Rahoy on Loch Sunart had been kidnapped and taken into the faery hill of Ben Iadain. The mother was able to appear to her husband in his dreams, telling him where she was and how to recover her. To do this, he had to go to the hill, taking with him the black silk handkerchief she had worn on their wedding day, with three knots tied upon it. Doing as she had instructed him, he successfully entered the hill and recovered his wife and child.[1]

Those taken into the faery hill often appear to other mortals to have died – but this is only an illusion, as is demonstrated in a number of Scottish stories in which the deceased person returns to a spouse or lover to explain their predicament and to seek help. This often happens in dreams, although a ghost-like apparition might also be seen. If the right steps are then taken, the individual will be able to return and often then will reveal that what had been buried was not their corpse at all, but a leaf, a stick or a log of alder wood. Sometimes, however, these pleas to

---

1 Campbell, *Superstitions,* 82; see too MacGregor, *Peat Fire Flame,* 6.

the survivors for redemption fail because the living fear to restore the 'dead' to life.[2]

I shall cite a number of failed dream contacts. A weaver from North Berwick, whose wife, after bearing two or three children, sadly died during the birth of their fourth child. The infant was saved, but the mother had expired in convulsions. As she was very disfigured after death, it became the local opinion that, due to some neglect by the midwife or by the women who ought to have watched the sick mother, she must have been carried off by the faeries and the ghastly corpse was merely a substitute put in the place of the body. The widower ignored this gossip, and, after mourning his wife for a year, decided to remarry so that he had a wife to look after his orphaned children. Shortly before the wedding, as he lay in his bed (awake as he supposed), he saw the figure of a female dressed in white, who had entered his cottage and was standing beside his bed. She was the very likeness of his late wife. He asked her to speak and was astonished to hear her say that she was not dead, but was instead held captive by the Good Neighbours. She told him that, if he still loved her, she could be recovered. She instructed him to gather all his neighbours and the parish priest and to disinter the coffin in which she was supposed to have been buried. After certain prayers had been said, she would leap out of the coffin and run with great speed around the church. The fastest runner in the village had to be there to pursue and catch her and the strongest man (the blacksmith) had to be there to hold her. The next morning the man was upset and puzzled by this dream, but didn't act on it. The wife appeared again the next night – and then on the third night she appeared with a sorrowful and displeased expression, complaining at his lack of love, and imploring him, for a final time, to do what she'd asked. If he now ignored her, she would never be able to visit the earth or communicate with him again. In order to convince him there was no delusion, he saw her pick up and breastfeed the

---

2 Campbell, *Superstitions,* 83, 86–87 & 89.

baby at whose birth she had died; she spilled also a drop or two of her milk on the poor man's bed-clothes, to convince him of the reality of the vision.

The next morning the terrified widower sought the priest's advice. He argued that the dream vision was real, but that it had been sent by the devil. Furthermore, as a minister of the church, he couldn't sanction the exhumation of a body in order to perform unauthorised rites. He advised the man to forget his dreams and instead to marry as rapidly as possible. The former widower did so and had no more dream visits from his deceased spouse.[3]

A man in Balemartin, on the south side of Tiree, whose wife had died in childbed, was sitting one night soon after with a bunch of keys in his hands. He saw his wife passing and repassing him several times. The following night she came to him in his dreams, and reproached him for not having thrown the bunch of iron keys at her, or between her and the door, so as to keep the faeries from taking her back with them. He asked her to come another night, but she said she could not, as the faery company she was with was moving that night to live under a hill far away. A third wife, taken in childbed, came to her husband in his sleep, and told him that, by drawing a furrow thrice round a certain hillock sunwise (*deiseal*) with the plough, he might recover her. He consulted his neighbours and, in the end, it was considered that it was best not to pay too much attention to a dream. He consequently didn't draw the furrow and never recovered his wife.[4]

Lastly, Katherine Fordyce of Unst, Shetland, died at the birth of her first child – or so it seemed to her family and friends. However, a neighbour's wife dreamed shortly after Katherine's death that she had come to her and said "I have taken the milk of your cow that you could not get, but it shall be made up to you; you shall have more than that, if you will give me what you will

---

3   Sir Walter Scott, *Letters on Demonology,* Letter V.
4   Campbell, *Superstitions,* 83 & 84.

know about soon." The dreamer wouldn't make the promise, because she had no idea what Katherine meant or what she was asking for, but soon afterwards she discovered that she was pregnant and understood that Katherine had referred to this child. The baby in due course was born and the mother named it Katherine Fordyce. After it was christened the 'trow-bound' Katherine re-appeared to the mother and told her all should prosper in her family whilst the child remained with it. Katherine also told the woman that she was herself quite comfortable among the trows, but could not escape unless somebody chanced to see her in the trow's hill and had presence of mind enough to bless her. She said her friends had failed to 'sain' her (guard her by charms) at the time of her own child's birth, and that was how she had fallen into the power of the trows.

Later, a man named John Nisbet saw Katherine. He was walking near her old home, when it seemed as if a hole opened in the side of a faery knowe. He looked in and saw Katherine inside, sitting in a "queer-shaped armchair and nursing a baby." There was a bar of iron stretched in front to keep her a prisoner. She was dressed in a gown which folk knew by John's description to have been her wedding-dress. He thought she said, "O Johnnie! what's sent you here?" to which he answered, "what keeps you here?" Katherine replied "I am well and happy but I can't get out, for I have eaten their food." Nisbet unfortunately did not know, or forgot to say, "Gude be aboot wis" (God bless us) – and Katherine was unable to give him a hint – so that, in a moment, the whole scene disappeared and she remained trapped in the hill.[5]

What emerges from these stories is a number of interesting facets to faery dream-communication. Firstly, and most significantly, it can be exploited by humans who have been taken into Faery, indicating that they somehow acquire faery powers simply by dint of being there with them. Secondly, it is a form of

---

5 Edmonston and Saxby, *The Home of a Naturalist,* 1888, 207; *County Folk-Lore* vol.3, 23–5.

contact that permits repeated, prolonged and detailed messages. These messages fail not because of communication breakdown – the medium seems highly effective – but because, for a variety of reasons, the recipient does not act on the information received.

Dream communications from Faery need not always concern the plight of abducted mortals. Sometimes, happier news or information is imparted. On Shetland, a girl out gathering shell fish on the beach noticed that a seal was watching her from just off-shore. Thinking little more of it, she sat in a cave mouth to eat her lunch and fell asleep there. A few months later it became clear that she was pregnant and, when the child was born, it was revealed whom the parent was: the child had flippers, instead of hands, and was plainly the off-spring of that seal. Fortunately for mother and baby, she dreamed that, if she went to a nearby 'geo,' a narrow rock inlet, she would find silver that would pay for her son's upbringing.[6]

Dreams might also be employed as a non-violent and yet compelling way of getting a human to remedy a trespass against the faeries. For example, a Scottish woman dreamed that she was visited by a strange female who complained that the stake used for tethering a cow was letting rain fall onto her child's cradle. The first night this happened, the woman dismissed it. After the same dream three nights in a row, she realised that it was a message, so she went, closed up the hole she'd made – and ended the dream warnings.[7]

---

6 Nicolson, *Shetland Folklore*, 88.
7 *www.tobarandualchais.co.uk*, Sept. 18th 1974.

Guidance through Dreams

Walter Evans Wentz concluded his study of the Celtic faery faith by stating that, amongst the phenomena that could not be explained by science, were "dream and trance states manifesting supernormal knowledge." Such communications are an important part of the human interaction with Faery across Britain.[1]

There is a famous English folk tale concerning a pedlar from Swaffham in Norfolk who had a dream that, if he went and stood on London Bridge, he would have very joyful news. As he had this dream a second and then third a third time, he decided to go to London. He stood on the bridge for several days without learning anything, when at last a shopkeeper, observing how the stranger had loitered there so long, neither offering anything for sale nor begging, asked him why he was there. The pedlar told him his errand, and was heartily laughed at by the shopkeeper, who said that, only the previous night, he'd dreamt that he was at a place called Swaffham in Norfolk, and that if only he dug under a great oak tree in an orchard behind a pedlar's house there, he would find a vast treasure. However, the place was utterly unknown to him, and he was not such a fool as to follow a silly dream. He advised the pedlar to forget about it too. The pedlar very quietly took in the details of the dream, and hastened home, where he found the treasure in his own orchard. If this was faery gold, which it may very well have been, the story indicates how the faeries may use dreams to guide and help us.[2]

---

1 Evans Wentz, *Fairy Faith*, 459; he went on to discuss dreams at length: 464–477 & 508–513.
2 John Rhys, *Celtic Folklore*, 466–467.

It seems that the faeries may send this knowledge unbidden to chosen beneficiaries or that they might assist individuals by answering questions posed to them. From Shetland there's the story of a faery shell (or bone cup) that was discovered on cliffs as the result of a dream. It had the power to cure jaundice if a complicated ritual involving fasting and silence was followed, central to which was water scooped from an easterly flowing well.[3]

In the Manx story of the *Fisherman and the Ben-Varrey*, a poor fisherman sees a mermaid in a dream, who advises him to dig near his house. He does so and finds a buried chest, "full of gold pieces of money, queer old coins with strange markings." He gives up working as a fisherman, thinking he has become wealthy for the rest of his life, but the money turns out to be worthless to him, as everyone in the local town is suspicious and refuses to take the Spanish gold, so the man and his wife have precious metals – but no income to buy food. As is often the case, faery money can be a curse as well as a favour.[4]

Bessie Skebister, of Orkney, was accused in March 1633 as a witch, in part because she had foreknowledge of events to come. She was condemned in court for being a "dreamer of dreams." Likewise, in Edinburgh in 1588 another accused witch, Alisoun Pearson, was said to have been granted, by the faeries, the power to know "what men may not know nor maidens dream."[5]

Recalling the possibility, mentioned earlier, that records of faery contact with humans whilst they are in their beds may in fact be instances of dream communication, I offer a few other examples of people being guided to wealth.

A miner at Mold was visited by a faery woman at night who woke him and encouraged him to follow her. She indicated to him where he should begin to excavate and the strata he would have to dig through in order to reach a rich vein of lead ore. The

---

3   B. Edmondston *Home of a Naturalist,* 1888, 215.

4   Dora Broome, *Fairy Tales from the Isle of Man,* 1968, 115.

5   Dalyell, *Darker Superstitions,* 470; J. MacDonald, 'Fauns & Fairies,' *Transactions of the Gaelic Society of Inverness,* vol.21, 1896, 275.

detailed geological information the woman supplied proved to be correct.[6] In 1820 a Pembrokeshire man was troubled at night by spirits making noise in his home. A local wise woman advised him to get up and follow them and, when he did, he was led to a hedge and beckoned to dig – where he discovered a silver inkstand buried in a pot.[7]

Sometimes, though, despite the visions and the guidance, the prospectors fail to find the hidden faery gold. What's not clear in such cases is whether this was just down to their poor excavating or because the faeries never meant them to have it in the first place. An Aberdeen resident called Walter Ronaldson had been visited by a faery in the form of a child twice a year over nearly thirty years. At Michaelmas in 1600 it came to him in bed, sitting on his chest and calling his name. Ronaldson was told that he was "under wraik" (subject to punishment) and that he had to go to a nearby house and dig, for he would find gold, silver and other valuables. Ronaldson dug as instructed, but found nothing. Despite his failure, he remained convinced the riches were present: "there is gold there, gif it were weel sought" he told a church court. In 1607, a woman called Susan Swapper, living at Rye in Sussex, was visited by four faeries at night. First, they told her to dig in a friend's garden within the town. She found nothing there but was "troubled by treasure" until the faeries told her to dig for another pot of gold, this time buried in a field outside the town. Once more, she did as she was instructed, but again failed to find any hoard.[8]

Our dreams reveal to us what we'd like to happen much more than they predict events to come. It seems that their use by faeries is exactly the same: they may tease us with visions of the wealth we'd like to find, or the lover we'd like to meet, far more than they foretell the consummation of our hopes.

---

6 'General Miscellany,' *Cardiff & Merthyr Guardian*, Nov. 30th 1850, 4.

7 'Pembrokeshire Fairy Lore,' *Cardiff Times*, June 11th 1904, 1.

8 Dalyell, *Darker Superstitions*, 1834, 531; *Selections from the Records of the Kirk Session, Presbytery and Synod of Aberdeen*, 1846, 184; D. Purkiss, *Troublesome Things*, 2000, 116.

PART THREE

Puzzling Faery Pastimes & Sports

We are very familiar indeed with the idea of faeries feasting and dancing, occupations which seem to take up a large amount of their time – judging by the frequency with which humans come across them so engaged – but they have other pastimes too which may surprise us, yet which can also make them seem very human indeed. In particular, and in opposition to their dances, these games reveal a competitive, even aggressive, side to Faery which we might be tempted to disregard. I have written before about their internal warfare; sport is but a sublimation of this.[1]

What is perhaps most puzzling about faery sports is what their existence reveals about our ignorance of Faery. Who are the competing sides? How are the competitions organised? When such essential elements are considered, we realise how little, in fact, we know about the faery lifestyle. Do they live in organised communities or states? Do their teams represent families, settlements or nations? How do they communicate their plans? We can guess, but we simply do not know any of these details. We know that games are played, but almost nothing more than that.

---

1   See my *How Things Work in Faery* (2021).

CURLING

It was reported in the late eighteenth century that, during freezing weather in the west of Scotland (at least), the faeries might be heard at night curling on every sizeable sheet of ice.[2]

On this sport, we might in passing merely remark that the faeries seem tied to the vagaries of the weather to enjoy it. Although they are able to control minor, local events, such as rain, fog and squalls of wind, larger climatic conditions appear to be beyond them. There is a distinct limit to their magical powers, making them as vulnerable to cold and rain as humans.

HURLING

In both Cornwall and (widely) in Ireland, huge hurling matches have been sighted, with hosts of players on either side. Coastal locations seem to be especially favoured for these: the earliest account of pixies being seen in Cornwall dates from August 1657 and is a description of a faery hurling match held in a field of corn at Boscastle. A large number of white figures were observed to be taking part and the game surged back and forth until apparently disappearing over a cliff. The crop, though, was left completely unmarked. Whether this implies something about the nature of faery physicality, faery movement (see next Part) or whether it just shows that they used magic to protect the corn is unknown. Another Cornish account concerns a man called Richard Vingoe who was pixie-led at Trevilly Cliffs south of Land's End. He followed an underground passage and eventually emerged into a pleasant country where he saw some men engaged in a game of hurling. He was about to join in when a woman he recognised (and whom he had thought was dead) stopped him and warned him of the dangers of getting trapped in Faery.[3]

---

2 R. Heron, *Observations Made on a Journey Through the Western Counties of Scotland,* 1793, 228.

3 Bottrell, *Traditions & Hearthside Stories of West Cornwall,* 1873, vol.2, 102.

In an Irish story, a man called Patch Gallagher is recruited to join one team in a vast *sidhe* hurling match which ranges over a full sixty miles of Connaught coastline. The puck was struck huge distances and the players travelled 'like the wind.' Evans Wentz also noted two Irish sightings of hurling matches. The particular interest of the Gallagher account is the fact that a mortal is recruited – the other side already have a man on their team apparently, "a fact which gives great advantage." The need for mortal aid is a common theme in faerylore – most notably the report from Wales that the *tylwyth teg* steal baby boys with a view to them leading their armies in battle.[4]

These instances of mortal involvement in faery games implicitly assume that the players will be of equal size. This raises the puzzling issue of faery stature: although they are often referred to as being small or child sized, human participation in sports indicates that the supernatural team members will be adult sized too. Of course, the faeries may simply have used glamour to swell themselves for the purposes of the game, or the human may magically have been shrunk. It's a puzzle we cannot resolve.

BALL GAMES

Various other types of ball game seem to be popular in Faery. One of the earliest British faery stories, that recounted by Gerald of Wales about the visit of a boy called Elidyr to a subterranean land, involves a game of catch with a golden ball, played with the son of the faery king.

From Neath in South Wales comes a curious tale in which the local faeries played marbles using small balls of clay taken from a nearby river bed. A girl who helped them make their marbles became very rich; a local farmer who grumbled that the water

---

4 Jeremy Harte, *Explore Fairy Traditions,* 2004, 140–141; Evans Wentz, *Fairy Faith,* 41 & 51.

was getting muddy so that his cattle couldn't drink it was met with derisive imitations of his complaints and laughter.[5]

From the Isle of Guernsey, we have an account of two faeries playing some sort of game involving a ball and bats – perhaps something akin to tennis. They were using two large stones as their bats and when one of the pair hit the ball so hard that it vanished, he stuck his bat in the ground and refused to carry on the game. The bat remains as the megalith called the *Palette es Fées*. In this case, the suggestion is that the faeries have the strength, if not the stature, of giants.[6]

The faeries also enjoy football. Evans Wentz recorded an Irish sighting of a soccer game, but far more interesting is a story from south Northamptonshire that tells of a man who joined a faery match (again implying physical parity between players). He was, perhaps, a little over-enthusiastic, as he kicked their ball so hard that it burst. He fainted and the fays vanished, but when he recovered, he found the deflated ball had been left behind and was full of gold coins.[7]

The first and last stories about ball games also have something to tell us about the faeries' puzzling attitude to gold. They know that the precious metal is something humans are obsessed with, yet for them it seems to have little value. Elidyr and his faery playmate use a golden ball – which seems impractically solid and heavy. On the one hand, this may indicate that the metal is little valued in Faery, yet its theft is pursued and punished. This is probably more to do with the violation of faery ethics than being a reflection of the price of the toy. In the Northamptonshire case, the gold coins left for the man are likely to signify the faeries' appreciation of his participation (and the value the gift will have to him) rather than any worth in their eyes.

---

5 Keightley, *Fairy Mythology*, 417.
6 E. MacCulloch, *Guernsey Folklore*, 1903, 127.
7 Sternberg, *Dialect & Folklore of Northamptonshire*, 137; Evans Wentz, *Fairy Faith*, 76.

HUNTING

The faeries love hunting with hounds, most particularly on the Isle of Man, where they are regularly heard at night coursing across the island. They are seen often dressed in green with red caps, in great numbers and accompanied by the loud sound of horns and cracking whips.[8]

The fact that faeries hunt must, of course, tell us something about their physical size. There is no indication in any of the folklore that they pursue anything different to the quarry hunted by humans. The Middle English poem *Sir Orfeo* sets out these assumptions clearly:

> "Oft in hot undertides [midday],
> Þe king o fairi, wiþ his rout,
> Come to hunt him al about,
> Wiþ dun [din], wiþ cri and bloweing,
> And houndes also wiþ him berkyng …
>
> And ich a faukon on hond bere,
> And riden hauking bi o rivere.
> Of game þai founde wel gode haunt –
> Malardes, hayroun, and cormeraunt.
> Þe foules of þe water ariseþ,
> Þe faucons hem wele deviseþ,
> Ich faucon his pray slouȝ [killed]."

Implicit in all of this description is the fact that the faery company are of human size, able to handle falcons and, equally, to cope easily with the prey they bring down.

---

8   See my *Manx Faeries* for more details.

HORSE RACING

As we'll discuss in Part Four, horses are often taken from humans' stables and are ridden at night until they're exhausted and foaming with sweat. It's very likely that the faeries are racing against each other as well as enjoying the sheer exhilaration of steeple-chasing over fields and hedges. Like hunting and games like football, it will be apparent that this pastime is not easily concealed from the mortal world. It requires space and can involve large numbers of competitors and spectators. Our idea of faeries as secretive and retiring may require revision.

Nonetheless, in direct contradiction of the preceding paragraphs, folklore almost always imagines horse-riding faeries and pixies to be diminutive. Rather than employing human saddles and bridles, they are renowned for plaiting manes into reins and stirrups so that they can manage the steeds. The inconsistency between accounts of faeries hunting and of faeries riding is a mystery that's very difficult to explain. We'll return to the subject in Part Four.

ROUGH AND TUMBLE PLAY

Even if no competitive game is involved, it's clear that the fays love to indulge in energetic and noisy play. Quite often, this is combined with mischief, disturbing human households with the noise they make. Poet Thomas Heywood referred to them "keeping Christmas gambols all night long," creating a racket that sounded as if furniture and pots were "about the Kitchen tost and cast/ Yet in the morning nothing found misplaced."

This sort of revelry is not just seasonal, though: poet Michael Drayton recorded in *The Muse's Elysium* how the faeries would scramble around rooms, overturning stools and tables. A Manx witness related how he saw the little folk playing on beached fishing boats, clambering about in the rigging with great laughter.

Eighteenth century writer George Waldron described another encounter on the island in which a man saw some boys playing in a field at about three or four o'clock in the afternoon when they should have been at school. He went to tell them off but they disappeared as he approached them across the open land.

Lastly, the *tylwyth teg* are known to engage in a number of playful pastimes. For example, they have been seen rolling head over heels down a mountain side for entertainment.[9]

9 'Gossiping Notes,' *Rhondda Leader,* Sept. 17th 1904, 7; Crofton Croker, 228; Keightley, *Fairy Mythology,* 417.

PART FOUR

The Mysteries of Faery Motion

Nowadays, it's all too easy to imagine faeries fluttering around with their butterfly or dragonfly wings. In fact, this image of their physique and of their means of locomotion has nothing to do with British tradition. The folklore conceptions of faery movement are, in fact, far more interesting than the idea of little winged beings. There are several forms of motion or travel, many quite surprising to us and challenging to our preconceptions.

Whirling Faes

Many faeries traditionally travel in whirlwinds, called in the Scottish Highlands the people's or host's breeze (*oiteag sluaigh*). The spinning air can act partly as a cover for human abductions, as a form of concealment, and as a means of inflicting harm on people, but in addition there are some indications that a spinning motion may be inherent in faery movement. It is well known from Scotland and Ireland, but is also reported from as far away as Cornwall and the Channel Islands.[1]

We have an early literary reference to this motion in the Scots drama *The Crying of Ane Playe – ane litill Interlude of the droichis* [dwarf's] *part of the play*. The character Harry Hobilschowe has long been with the faeries in Syria but is now returning home to Scotland, travelling, we are told, "with the quhorle wind."

Later Scottish tradition states that the faery folk of the island of Lewis, known as *muintir Fhionlaidh* ('Finlay's Folk) travel around in whirlwinds on calm days and will carry people short distances if they come across them asleep in their path. A common curse in the area was "May you get the lifting of the Finlay people." In the region of Ben Nevis and Glencoe, it was believed that the faeries went abroad at the Spring equinox, travelling in dust eddies on land and in the spindrift over the sea. They swirl about in squalls and water spouts and can cause sickness and check the growth of plants. In Gloucestershire, too, it is said that tiny whirlwinds in the road are the faeries passing; whirls of dried leaves in the Forest of Dean have the same explanation. In North-East Scotland, a small whirl of dust in the wind is called 'a furl o' fairies ween' (a whirl of the faeries' wind).[2]

---

1   MacPhail, 'Fairylore from the Hebrides,' *Folklore*, vol.7, 1896, 402.
2   MacPhail, 'Fairylore from the Hebrides,' *Folklore*, vol.7, 1896, 402; L. Spence, *Fairy Tradition in Britain*, 65; A. Stewart, *Twixt Ben Nevis & Glencoe*, 1885, 213; R. Palmer, *Folklore of Gloucestershire*, 1994, 145; L. Spence, *Fairy Tradition in Britain*, 65.

My earliest folklore account of an actual encounter with whirling faeries comes from Worcestershire and dates to before 1793. A man working in a field at Upton Snodsbury helped a faery by mending a broken implement. This is a common incident and, in this case, a 'bilk' or chair needed repair. The thankful faery rewarded the human with food (as, again, is the usual outcome) but in this instance, rather than leaving the gift for the person to find, he "danced round him till he *wound* him down into a cave, where he was treated with plenty of biscuits and wine."[3]

A second case comes from mid-Wales in 1862. Two carters, David Evans and Evan Lewis, were travelling from Brecon to New Quay in Ceredigion with wagon loads of timber. At Maestwynog, one August afternoon, they saw some small people climbing to the top of a hill. The group danced in a circle there for a while, but then began to spiral into the centre, "like a gimblet screw." Finally, successively, the figures disappeared into the ground. The dancing beforehand reinforces the sense that circular motion may be especially fay, but this sighting takes matters further – as does a Manx example, in which a very troublesome buggane was described as "whirling like a spinning wheel" on top of a mountain.[4]

The Jersey faeries travel in whirlwinds and use them to carry off people and animals. A victim can be released by throwing a bonnet, left shoe, knife or some mole hill earth into the eddy. The same is the case in the Scottish Highlands: a man's wife was taken for seven years by the *sith* folk. One day, he was out cutting thatch when a whirlwind passed. He threw a handful of dust into the eddy and his wife appeared, believing she had only been absent one day.[5]

North Cornish writer Enys Tregarthen recounted the story of a woman out with her baby in a potato field when she was caught

---

3   Jacob Allies, *British, Roman and Saxon Antiquities,* 308.
4   Ceredig Davies, *Folklore,* 128; Broome, *Fairy Tales,* c.2 – 'Old Nance and the Buggane'.
5   J. L'Amy, *Jersey Folklore,* 1927, 24; E. Murray, *Scottish Gaelic Texts,* vol.7, *Tales from Highlands Perthshire,* 157, no.57.

in the dust of a whirlwind. When the eddy had passed, she saw that her child had been replaced by a wizened old creature. She cared for the changeling, hoping that its good treatment would win the return of her own child, but it pined away and died and she never recovered her own baby.[6]

A further case from south west Scotland seems to underline the fact that a corkscrew motion comes naturally to faery-kind. A suspected changeling was tied up by the human parents and was held over a smoky fire in a sieve. The measure worked, for the faery cursed and then "gaed whirling up among the reek like a corkscrew and out of the lumhead ..." (went whirling up through the smoke and out by the chimney).[7]

Much more recent sightings suggest that this corkscrew motion was far from unusual. A woman from Monmouthshire twice saw faeries – in 1945 and 1949 – and each time they first appeared to her as a whirling shape before the individual faery became visible. The fays have also been seen to "spin round and round at a tremendous speed, and then vanish at the peak." The spinning motion can be imparted to objects they're standing on as well (such as a bowl of tulips).[8]

The more traditional whirlwinds are still seen too, out on country roads but also now in modern urban environments. An art school student from North Carolina saw a figure inside a tiny vortex only one foot high and a factory security guard saw faeries in dust devils as a child.[9]

One perhaps significant thing that we don't know about the faeries' spinning motion is its direction. As we saw in Part Two – in the case of the Highland husband who was asked by his wife to rescue her from the faery knoll by ploughing sunwise (*deisal*) around the hill – in faery matters the direction of movement

---

6 E. Tregarthen, *North Cornwall Fairies & Legends,* 185 'Fairy Whirlwind.'

7 J. Maxwell Wood, *Witchcraft & Superstitious Record in the South West District of Scotland,* 1911, 167; R. Trotter, *Galloway Gossip,* 1901, 288.

8 *Seeing Fairies,* 47, 106, 155 & 212

9 *Seeing Fairies* 229 and *Fairy Census* 346 & 419

may have magical significance. Frequently, water from a south-flowing stream is required for cures and, in many charms against the faeries, clockwise motion is prescribed as a key part of the spell.[10]

It would be very interesting to know, therefore, whether the whirlwinds and the corkscrewing faeries travelled clockwise or not. A hint that this could be important comes from an incident reported from Shetland. A man out early one day saw two 'grey men' (in other words, trows) approaching a cow lying down in a field. They walked up to it and then ran away from it backwards; the cow immediately stood up and followed them to the limit of its tether. It died later that day, a clear sign that it had been 'taken under the hill.' This backwards running, against the normal direction of travel, might imply that doing something 'anti-clockwise' is important to the working of faery magic. This appears to be confirmed by a passage in a manuscript written in the early eighteenth century by John Bell, minister of the church at Gladsmuir, near Prestonpans in East Lothian. He warned against using charms, spells and verses, amongst which he numbered "going backwards."[11]

To summarise – in the past, spinning appears to have been considered essentially faery – so much so that the magic necessary to achieve it might even be imparted to whoever or whatever is carried along in the faery eddy: for example, a farmer living on the island of Tiree saw one of his sheep being whirled up into the sky by a gust of wind. He was so certain that the faeries had done this that, when the sheep came to be slaughtered, he refused to eat any of its meat – plainly because he considered it tainted in some manner. What's most curious is that spells cast by the faeries also seem to partake of this swirling motion. In a

10 See, for example, in my *Darker Side of Faery* and *Faeries & the Natural World* (both 2021).

11 J. Saxby, *Shetland Traditional Lore,* 1932, 161; J. Bell, *A Discourse of Witchcraft,* 1705, cited in R. Laws, *Memorialls,* 1818, lxxvi, footnote.

Scottish witch trial from 1647, a woman called Barbara Parish was accused of consorting with the faeries and of killing John Giffen's wife by "putting the wirlle wind in her hasse [throat] that made her rattle til death."[12]

---

12 A. Macdonald, 'A Witchcraft Case of 1647,' *Scots Law Times*, April 10th 1937, 77–78.

Flying with the Sluagh

The *sluagh* are the faery host in the folklore of the Scottish Highlands. In this region of Britain people may be abducted either by being taken inside a faery hill or by being snatched up into the air and carried away with the *sluagh* as they fly over the land. This experience of *falbh air an t-sluagh* (going with the host) typically involves being carried great distances at night. A dismal sound like the rushing of wind, carrying the sound of wailing voices, precedes the sluagh's arrival and individuals who have flown with them are left pale, bewildered and awestricken by the experience. This is because they are transported at great height through the sky and – it seems – at great speed.[1]

The *sluagh* is known by several names in Gaelic, all of which indicate something about the nature and origin of the faery host. British authority Lewis Spence called them the *sluagh eotrom*, meaning the light or aery host, a term which must reflect their ability to fly, or even their corporeal nature. The Reverend Robert Kirk made a distinction between the *sluagh saoghalta* and the *sluagh sith*. The latter is the 'faery host' and the former the 'secular' or 'worldly' host. Bearing in mind that the Gaelic word 'sluagh' more broadly denotes a people or population, this makes sense of what Kirk says next "Souls goe to the *Sith* when dislodged." In other words, once earthly people die, they join the faery multitude instead, travelling freely through the air beyond the constraints of their mortal bodies. Likewise, Evans Wentz referred to the faeries of the air or the 'spirit host,' which

---

1   J.L. Campbell & T.H. Hall, *Strange Things*, 2006, 267, no.37 & 268, no.39; G. Sutherland, *Folklore Gleanings ... from the Far North*, 1932, 27; MacGregor, *Peat Fire Flame*, 93.

he stated were distinct from the *sith* who lived underground. Kirk may be correct in treating the *sluagh* as akin to the hosts of the dead, but all our direct evidence relates to the kidnapping and return of living persons.[2]

We can learn something more about the nature of the faery host and the process of being snatched up by them from the experience of John MacPhee of Uist. McPhee was outside his house one night when he heard a sound like the breaking of the sea approaching from the West (a direction intimately associated with the host). He saw a mass of small men coming his way and suddenly felt hot, as if a crowd of people had surrounded him and were pressing in, breathing upon him. Then he was snatched up into the air and carried at great speed to the graveyard at Dalibrog, seventeen miles from his home. For a moment or two MacPhee was set down, and the sensation of heat left him. However, the host soon returned, he felt hot again, and was carried back through the sky to his home. After this experience, MacPhee became sickly and thin. The man clearly suffered some of the typical physical after-effects of close contact with faeries and, although the author of the account referred to the host as 'the dead,' the evidence of their living physicality seems very much to contradict this description. The same corporal reality is demonstrated in several cases of people who were not only carried off repeatedly by the *sluagh*, but physically mistreated by them, being dragged through muddy bogs. Combined with the sheer terror of the kidnapping and flight, this manhandling can leave human victims terrorised and in extreme exhaustion and may prove fatal. Such unfortunate individuals will often refuse to go outside at night when the *sluagh* are most likely to be abroad.[3]

---

2 Spence, *British Fairy Tradition*, 60; Kirk, *Secret Commonwealth*, 'Succinct Accompt,' 9 (10); Evans Wentz, *Fairy Faith*, 104 & 108, fn.1; on faeries and the dead see my *Faery* c.3; on the physical nature of faeries, my *Faery Lifecycle*.

3 Campbell & Hall, *Strange Things*, 297, no.52; Watson, 'Celtic Mythology,' *Celtic Review*, vol.5, 1908–9, 60; Campbell, *Superstitions*, 70; A. Carmichael, *Carmina Gadelica*, vol.2, 357; MacGregor, *Peat Fire Flame*, 90–91.

THE NATURE OF THE SLUAGH

The mass nature of the *sluagh's* travel is apparent; so too is their resemblance to other flying creatures as they pass over the land. They travel in a multitude – according to one Scottish witness moving "in great clouds, up and down the face of the world like starlings." Dun Gharsain, at Bracadale on the Isle of Skye, was once well known as a 'bower' or dwelling of the *sith* people, from which they emerged at Halloween, like "starlings swarming from their cave." A man from Mingulay who managed to get trapped on a cliff ledge whilst out catching birds was saved by the *sluagh*, who appeared like a flock of birds and lifted him to the cliff top. When visiting the island of Barra, Evans Wentz was told that the host went about at midnight, travelling in fine weather against the wind like a 'covey of birds.'[4]

We shall return again later to these comparisons between the *sluagh* in flight and flocks or swarms of animals.

THE MANNER OF FLIGHT

The *sluagh* can travel over the countryside in a number of ways. They can use the whirlwinds that have just been described; an example is that of a Tiree man called Black Donald of the Host (*Domhnull du an t-sluaigh*) who was carried away from a field he was ploughing by an eddy. Its approach was, to a degree, disguised by the fact that arrived as part of a heavy shower of rain that blew in from the west (the faery compass point again). Donald was absent for a whole day, telling on his return at his initial terror when he was transported across the sea and how he had had to kill a cow with an arrow. The use of squalls by the *sluagh* seems quite common.[5]

---

4 Watson, 'Celtic Mythology,' *Celtic Review,* vol.5, 1908–09, 59; Evans Wentz, *Fairy Faith,* 108; *Carmina Gadelica,* vol.2, 308; *Tobar an Dulchais,* August 1970.

5 Campbell, *Superstitions,* 69, also 71 & 72.

The Scottish witch suspect, Bessie Dunlop, attested to the same process. She had been visited by twelve faery folk who left her in "ane hideous uglie sowche of wind." A *sowche* is a sough, a rushing or whistling. This suggests violence, as does the experience of one Patie McNicol, from Sheardale, Clackmannanshire. One evening, he heard the sound of sighing around his head and was then suddenly lifted up and carried through the sky at terrible speed. He was found on top of the Ochil Hills the next day, cold and hungry, and never recovered: instead, he "dwindled like melting snow until he died."[6]

The previous two examples imply that the *sluagh* travels in a rushing gale, but in the Scottish Highlands these eddies are also called the *oiteag sluagh*, the host's breeze or puff of wind, suggestive of something much gentler. This seems to be confirmed by an incident that took place in the 1870s at Houstry near Dunbeath in Caithness. Sandy Gunn left his home one summer morning to visit his sister in Latheronwheel (*Latharn a' Phuill*), which is only four miles away – a walk of an hour or so. He didn't arrive until the middle of the next day, saying that, when he had reached the hill called Cnoc-an-Crask, he had felt a gentle breeze, lost his footing and had been carried up into the air. He found himself flying across the country all day and all night with the faeries, ultimately being set down at the same spot the next day.[7]

We tend to imagine that a victim is bodily snatched up by the *sith* grabbing their arms or torso, but a strange report from Bowden in Roxburghshire describes a rather different process. A man called Ronaldson was out early one morning when "he was startled at feeling something like a rope of straw passed between his legs and himself borne swiftly away upon it ...". He was set down four miles away on the Eildon Hills and, taking his chance, he invoked god's name and felt the 'rope' break. In fact,

6 Pitcairn, *Ancient Criminal Trials,* vol.1, 49–58 & vol.2(1) 25; *Scottish Journal,* vol.2, 1848, 274 or Westwood, *Lore of Scotland,* 114.
7 G. Sutherland, *Folklore Gleanings ... from the Far North,* 1932, 28.

as we shall see, abduction by the host is much more likely to be a matter of 'glamour' than any physical kidnapping. Thus, the impression of faery flight that we glean from the stories is that it is an intangible, magical ability and that it can transferred to any that they choose to have accompany them. This not only includes human victims but also horses and hounds used for hunting.[8]

All the flights seen so far appear to have taken place physically unaided, but the host can also travel on objects which have been imbued with their faery glamour, such as bulrushes ('bulwands'), docks, ragwort and withered grass stems. For example, Scottish poet Alexander Montgomerie described the times of year "When our good nighbours doe ryd … Some buckled on a bunwand, and some on a been" in his verse *The Flyting Between Montgomerie and Polwart* (1585). Handy items can be rendered airborne by means of a simple spell. Various forms of words are recorded – simply naming the location to which you want to go might be enough in some cases. By way of illustration, from Cornwall we hear of a grocer's boy who'd made a delivery at Polperro and was walking back home to Porthallow. He saw some people ahead of him in the road, one of whom shouted "I'm for Porthallow." The boy responded with the same words – and found himself flying through the air with the pixies.[9]

On other occasions, a magic formula is required to get an object into the air, and the commonest of which we hear is the cry of "Horse and hattock!" It's never made clear why these words are used, but we can hazard a few guesses. As just stated, the faes can enchant plant stems to ride like horses through the air. Now, a hattock is no longer an everyday word in English, but it means a sheaf or stook of corn, so perhaps what we have here is a spell to turn a wheat or barley stem into a mount. There is of

---

8 W. Henderson, *Notes on the Folklore of the Northern Counties*, 1866, 159; Westwood, *Lore of Scotland*, 220; A. Carmichael, *Carmina Gadelica*, vol.2, 257.

9 T. Quiller Couch, 'Folklore of a Cornish Village,' *Notes & Queries*, 1st series, no.11, 398.

course an evident connection with witches' broomsticks here, although it seems the faeries have a great deal more choices of flight available to them.

What's more, the faeries may move around using items in which the magical power of flight has been permanently invested. This is illustrated by a story from Herefordshire, in which a boy lost in woods finally comes across a cottage and is taken in by the two women living there. Later that night they put on white caps and fly off to a faery dance. He uses a third spare cap to follow them, although he's later admonished by them for his impudence.[10]

Humans who witness faery flight are also able to imitate the faeries' actions and thereby transfer their magic power to other items on which to fly, such as ploughs or loom beams. However, this has to be done with care. This may be illustrated by the experience of the laird of Dunblane, who was returning home late one night when, near the Burn of Menstry, he saw a group of small women dressed in green collecting 'windle straes' (dry grass stems) which they were tying into bunches. The laird was leaning against a plough, watching the women, when one of them approached him and invited him to do like them and join them in enjoying a good supper. The woman then got astride her bundle and, on saying "Brechin to the Brithul" flew up into the air. The laird straddled the plough, did the same and joined the company at a house where they ate and drank unseen. Then they said "Cruinan to the Dance" and flew out through the keyhole "like a sough of wind." The man was so impressed by this that he congratulated the plough he was sitting on – which broke the spell. He descended to earth where he'd started and as far from home as ever. A Manx weaver had a very similar experience, riding on his loom beam with the faeries until they approached a precipice – which made the man bless himself; instantly, the

---

10   Leather, *Folklore of Herefordshire,* 176.

beam sank to the ground and the weaver had to carry it home on his shoulder.[11]

In point of fact, though, physical travel is not actually necessary at all, for a man in Sutherland was taken in spirit one night by the *sluagh*, even after his friends had forcibly restrained his body to try to prevent his abduction. This case highlights another matter, which is that, if a person is called to travel with the *sluagh,* there is no denying that summons. In a second case, for instance, a man on Skye saw the host approaching and begged his friend to hold him tightly to prevent his abduction. Despite the friend's best efforts, the victim began to 'hop and dance' before rising off the ground and being carried a couple of miles. Sometimes a person picked up by the *sluagh* will simply disappear for a while; on other occasions, they may appear to die to their friends and family whilst their living body is carried off. An example of this is the story of a newly-married young man from Islay who was snatched up in an eddy by the 'Lady of the Emerald Isle.' His wife believed she had buried him, but he appeared to her one night and explained that he was alive and well and that she had only buried a 'stock,' an oak log.[12]

Stories of involuntary flight with the faeries come from Wales, too. They make quite explicit the fact that flight is very rarely pleasant for the human taken along. The *tylwyth teg* will offer human victims the choice to travel either above, in the middle of or below the wind. Above is a giddy and terrible sensation, whilst below doesn't involve the terror of great height but (obviously) involves being dragged through bush and brake. This latter was plainly the experience of one man whose case was described by the Reverend Edmund Jones in the late eighteenth century.

---

11 *Old Lore Miscellany,* vol.5, 16; W. Marwick, *Folklore of Orkney & Shetland,* 1975, 35; J. Monteath, *Dunblane Traditions,* 1835, 101; *Yn Lioar Manninagh,* vol.3.

12 Mackay, 'Fairies in Sutherland,' *Celtic Magazine,* vol.9, 1884, 207; Aubrey, *Miscellanies,* 149; Campbell, *Popular Tales,* vol.4, 340; A. MacGregor, *The Peat Fire Flame,* 1937, 94.

A hunting party visited a pub kept by Richard the tailor, "one who resorted to the company of fairies." One of the group went outside to relieve himself and was snatched up by a passing faery band. He was with them all night, being carried all the way from Monmouthshire to Newport and back again. When he reappeared the next morning, he "looked like he'd been pulled through thorns and briars." He felt very ill and said that for part of his journey he had been insensible. Evidently, he had been travelling below the wind. Another man Jones mentions was carried in the sky forty miles to Newport and back: the terror of the journey reduced him to insensibility and, on his return, he looked "bad" – a fine understatement, we may suspect. Given that the mere experience of being taken by the faeries can be an unpleasant experience, it's hardly surprising that being kidnapped by flying faes generally proves deeply distressing.[13]

All in all, the impression we gain from most reports of the *sluagh's* aerial motion is that it is nimble, rapid *and* effortless. We read earlier about them travelling *against* the wind, apparently unperturbed by adverse weather conditions. It's odd, therefore, to discover one folklorist describing how on "bad nights, the hosts shelter themselves behind the little russet docken stems and little yellow ragwort stalks." This leaves the strong impression that, whilst their magic can conjure up whirling winds, it is itself weak in the face of nature's own tempests.[14]

REASONS FOR FLIGHT

The reason for the host's aerial journeys seems to be uniformly malicious. The primary aim is to abduct humans – for fun, for company or, perhaps, as lovers. Secondary purposes include shooting elf-bolts at people and livestock or stealing human property – usually food and drink. From this it will be evident

---

13 Jones, *The Appearance of Evil,* no.68; Jones, *Aberystruth,* 70 & 81; on the effects of faery abduction, see my *Darker Side of Faery* c.4 & *Faery* c.12.
14 A. Carmichael, *Carmina Gadelica,* vol.2, 357.

that transporting loads through the air presents them with no challenges at all.[15]

That carrying humans or livestock poses no problems is demonstrated by the fact that people may be carried a short distance of just a few miles, or they may be carried away over the ocean to other islands or even different countries (although much more local journeys are more typical). Evans Wentz, for instance, describes men carried from one end of the Hebrides to another (over one hundred miles). In a second example, a sailor on the island of St Martin's, off the Ross-shire coast, was carried by a rainstorm ten miles to another island and back; a man with the second sight on Coll who regularly travelled with the *sluagh* was one time taken to a rock in the sea and kept there for two hours before being returned to the mainland. Some trows flew all the way from Shetland to Norway to abduct a newly married woman, for example, and some faeries in Moray conveyed a man to Paris. Likewise, a king's daughter could perfectly easily be abducted from Paris to Benbecula and a Spanish princess carried to Kiel on the Morvern peninsula in Argyll.[16]

Other reasons for the *sluagh* to fly are to hunt with hounds and hawks across the land and to travel to war with enemy hosts. Much as with the sporting activities described in the previous Part, who their foes might be and what the grounds for their hostilities could be are unknown to us. Nevertheless, there are several Scottish accounts of the opposing hosts battling in the sky on cold and frosty nights (and especially at Halloween), leaving pools of blood (*fuil nan* sluagh) on the ground in the morning as testimony to casualties inflicted. Indeed, it seems that another reason for carrying off humans is to lead the faery armies against each other. These battles are rarely seen, but the sound of the hosts' armour is said to be a rustling, like "the sound

---

15 Monteath, *Dunblane Traditions*, 101.

16 Campbell, *Superstitions*, 69–73 & 87; Evans Wentz, 106; *Old Lore Miscellany*, vol.5, 16; Mackenzie, *Book of Arran*, 258 & 268; MacGregor, *Peat Fire Flame*, 90–91.

of a breeze disturbing withered reeds." This is a curious simile, ill-suited to mortal conflict, and it relates back to the discussion in the previous section as to whether the host travels as a gale or a gentle zephyr.[17]

Flight might be used to hunt, to fight or to take people and animals, but the experience of flight itself might be sufficiently unpleasant to be used as a punishment in itself for those who have aggrieved the *sluagh*. A minister in Ross-shire in Scotland had spoken in a slighting manner of the faeries and they exacted their revenge by picking him up and carrying him head over heels through the air.[18]

Rarely, people enjoy the experience of flight, as with the man from Tiree called Black Donald, whose only regret over his aerial adventure with the host was being made to kill the cow on Skye. Even more rarely, some individuals may be carried by the host at their own request. For example, one Calum Clever of Connal Ferry, near Benderlock, was an accomplished singer and (it was inferred) a favourite of the faeries as a result. One time he was sent on an errand to Fort William and made the journey so quickly that he could only have managed it with the host's help. It has been reported that, on the Shetland islands, those who are on good terms with the trows "by special indulgence, have been transported into the air, wherever occasion served, from one island to another." Such a case seems to have involved a piper from Reay on the mainland. He spent many days with the faeries, improving his piping skills and playing for them and, in return, they would carry him speedily wherever he wanted to go, so he was always on time to provide entertainment at weddings and was never wet or muddy from bad weather.[19]

---

17 A. Carmichael, *Carmina Gadelica*, vol.2, 257; Watson, 'Celtic Mythology,' *Celtic Review*, vol.5, 1908–9, 59–60; Evans Wentz, 91; MacGregor, *Peat Fire Flame*, 91 & 88.

18 Campbell, *Popular Tales*, 79.

19 MacGregor, *Peat Fire Flame*, 92; Campbell, *Superstitions*, 72; S. Hibbert, *Description of the Shetland Isles*, 444; Sutherland, *Folklore Gleanings*, 27.

To conclude, then, a few humans are naturally exhilarated by the experience of flight and the novelty of visiting strange places in far lands. Others are keen to try it at first, but then find it's not anywhere near as enjoyable as they had hoped. For most, given the typical altitude and acceleration, it is shattering and sometimes mortal.

ESCAPING FLIGHT

The accounts so far, especially that of the man taken despite the best efforts of his friends to prevent it, might suggest that the *sluagh* can neither be escaped or resisted. This is not the case, fortunately. Very simple measures can defeat them. Two abductions of women on the Isle of Arran were prevented by means of casting a reaping hook up into the "multitude of little people" passing over his head, looking like a bee swarm. Being iron, this instantly released the captives who were being carried away. Knives and other steel implements will work just as well as will a left shoe. Likewise, the use of a variety of charms and of Christian blessings is effective: a Shetland man flew with the trowie host on a rush by imitating their spell ("Up hors, up hedik, up well ridden bolwind") and he found himself taken with them to a cottage where a woman was in labour. The plan was to take the new mother if she sneezed three times and no one 'sained' or protected her. She sneezed, but the man carried off by the trows instinctively said 'bless you' and so prevented her abduction.[20]

Being carried off by the *sluagh* seems, in fact, to have been a common enough danger in the Scottish Highlands for it to be incorporated into a prayer to St Brigit asking for her protection against a range of dangers, that included fire, drowning and that:

---

20 Mackenzie, *Book of Arran,* 258 & 268; MacGregor, *Peat Fire Flame,* 93–94; Campbell, *Superstitions,* 87; Nicolson, *Shetland Folklore,* 82; *Old Lore Miscellany,* vol.5, 16.

"Cha tog siodhach mi,
Cha tog sluagach mi."

"No seed of the faery host shall lift me;
Nor seed of airy host shall lift me."[21]

The foregoing are magical defences; physical means of resistance tend to be much less certain and far riskier. Some men were tending the herds at Cornaigbeg Farm on Tiree when they heard something passing them on the road. It sounded like a flock of sheep passing, but one of the dogs became very agitated and chased after it. Eventually the poor hound returned – it had lost all its hair and was torn and bloody, dying soon afterwards.[22]

---

21 Carmichael, *Carmina Gadelica,* vol.3, 161.
22 Campbell, *Popular Superstitions,* 144.

Faery Motion

The faeries can fly, and they can travel as or within a whirlwind. They can also move about in much more prosaic ways, such as walking, running or riding. Over and above this, though, there are other, yet stranger, reports.

FAERIES ON FOOT

Evans Wentz recorded that the normal means of the *sith* getting around was walking, just like humans. We know for certain that the brownies get around on foot. For instance, there's a widely known story of a devoted domestic sprite at Cash in Lowland Scotland who walked daily from his dwelling to the house to which he was attached, crossing a stream by stepping stones on the way. One day, when the weather was bad and the water levels had risen, the people in the house didn't expect to see him because the river was too treacherous to cross – but the brownie impressed them with his commitment to his duties by walking a long distance out of his way in order to cross the torrent by a bridge. Plainly, if levitation or flight had been an option, he would have used them.[1]

The same logic seems to apply when the faeries decide to abandon a place. The Manx little folk decided to quit Colby after a flour mill was built there. Disturbed by the human intrusion and constant noise, they were seen early one morning climbing up into the mists and solitude of the mountain glens, with all their household goods on their backs. Once again, if less strenuous means of removal were available, one might presume they would have employed them.[2]

---

1 Evans Wentz, *Fairy Faith*, 108; H. Aitken, *A Forgotten Heritage*, 37.
2 A. Herbert, *The Isle of Man*, 1909, 177.

FLYING FAERIES?

The nearest we come in the folklore record to some indication of winged flight is a couple of Victorian descriptions of encounters. An example from West Yorkshire dates to about 1850. A man called Henry Roundell, of Washburn Dale near Harrogate, got up early one day to hoe his turnips. When he reached the field, he was astonished to discover that every row was being hoed by a host of tiny men in green, all of them singing in shrill cracked voices "like a lot of field crickets." As soon as he tried to climb over the stile into the field, they fled 'like flocks of partridges.' Another nineteenth century account from nearby Ilkley tells of a crowd of faeries surprised whilst bathing in the local spa baths. The caretaker of the wells cried out in astonishment and "away the whole tribe went, helter skelter, toppling and tumbling, head over heels, heels over heeds, and all the while making a noise not unlike a disturbed nest of young partridges." As they fled there was a whirring noise, which sounds very like startled wings, but we are told that "the fairies were "bounding over the walls like squirrels." In fact, if you look closely at both accounts, there's no suggestion that they actually flew away like birds – merely that the startled commotion sounded similar to this.[3]

Although no actual winged flight is involved, flocks of birds are a common comparator from groups of faeries in motion. A man at Benbecula in the Hebrides heard the *sluagh* go over – it sounded to him 'like a flock of plovers.' As we've already seen, the movement of the host has often been likened to that of starlings.[4] Similar accounts come from the Isle of Man; one concerns a changeling. The nature of the child was revealed to his family by a visiting tailor and they took the necessary steps to banish the faery infant, building up the fire in order to scare the supernatural away. The 'baby' leapt out of his cradle when he saw

---

3 Roberts *Folklore of Yorkshire* 60; Crofton Croker, *Fairy Legends,* 86.
4 Campbell, *Strange Things,* no.38; Carmichael, *Carmina Gadelica,* vol.2, 330.

what was being prepared and ran out of the house. The mother then saw "a flock of low-lying clouds shaped like gulls chasing each other away up Glen Rushen," along with whistles and wicked laughter. Her true son then returned to her. Some other Manx faeries, seen one moonlit night, looked like nothing so much as a black rain cloud. Scores of the little folk were in motion; although the witness followed them, they kept between twenty and thirty yards ahead of him, shrinking in size until they disappeared. The *sluagh* has also been seen in Scotland like a dark cloud, making a terrible sound.[5]

The evasiveness and the cloud-like quality in the Manx encounter are fairly typical of accounts. Very frequently the faes are said to behave and look like insects. Manx folklorist Dora Broome twice described the faeries as "like a swarm of bees."[6] Another Manx writer also said that the faery host sounded first like humming bees.[7] A man on Arran working in a field saw something like a swarm of bees pass over him. Throwing up his (iron) reaping hook, he found his wife drop to the ground before him; the faeries had been in the process of abducting her. This was a common simile. In John Dryden's play *An Evening's Love* a magician declares:

> "I have been making there my magical operations ... and, to perform it rightly, have been forced to call up spirits of several orders: And there they are humming like a swarm of bees, some stalking about upon the ground, some flying, and some sticking upon the walls like rear-mice [bats]."[8]

Typically, then, the faeries move through the air, and they move *en masse*. A final, slightly different, example of this is the

---

5 Morrison, 'A Manx Changeling Story,' *Folklore*, vol.21, 1910, 472; W.H. Gill, 'Facts & Fancies of Fairyland,' *Mannin*, vol.2, 1913; Campbell & Hall, *Strange Things*, 268, no.40.

6 Broome, *Fairy Tales*, 67 & *More Fairy Tales*, 40.

7 Sophia Morrison, *Manx Fairy Tales*, 'Billy Beg, Tom Beg & the Fairies.

8 MacKenzie, *Book of Arran*, 267; Dryden, *An Evening's Love*, 1668, Act V, scene 1.

experience of a man from Shetland, who was travelling home at night over the hills at Coningsburg when he was surrounded by trows in the form of mice. There were so many around him, so thickly on the ground, that he said he couldn't have put down a pin without hurting one. This went on until dawn when he reached a small stream, at which moment the mass of mice all vanished. A curious sequel followed. Although the innumerable rodents had been surprising and inconvenient, they hadn't been dangerous. However, on the bridge over the brook there were three knights. The man was so astonished, he uttered a curse, and the three men also disappeared – with a bang and a flash of blue flame.[9]

What does this tell us? It seems to make clear that, in some parts of Britain, the experience of encountering the fae is not a matter of meeting an individual who is the human sized – whether that's an adult or, more often, a child. Rather, we are dealing with a species who naturally move about in hosts, wheeling about much like large flocks of birds – or perhaps clouds of midges or flies. Consistent with this, they are small – or even tiny.

Some faeries (especially pixies) are shapeshifters and can transform themselves into birds, but this is a rare ability and is definitely not a widespread means of travel. Others – it would appear – have a movement akin to that of a bird, yet they are not flying with wings, as such. Perhaps rather more often than fluttering, some (literary) faeries are taken to 'teleport' from one spot to another: witness Ariel in *The Tempest*, putting a girdle about the earth in forty minutes.

SKIPPING AND SPEEDING

"And in the fields of martial Cambria ...
Where light foot fairies skip from bank to bank."[10]

---

9   Johnston, *Old Lore Miscellany of Orkney, Shetland & Caithness*, vol.7–8, 198.
10   *The Tragedy of Locrine*, 1594, attributed to Shakespeare.

Some authorities believe that faery motion is typified by its great speed, which is achieved without perceptible effort. A man who met some Scottish faeries on Halloween described to poet James Hogg how "their motions were so quick and momentary he could not well say what they were doing."[11] Supporting this, an account from Craignish describes faery motion as being very swift – yet without perceptible effort. Their hands and feet apparently move so quickly that they are virtually invisible. They appeared to glide very rapidly through the air without touching the ground.[12] Nonetheless, another witness reported how she saw a trow getting about by skipping – backwards, something which sounds slow and ungainly.[13]

FLOATING

> "Oh, band of mischievous fairies,
> That flicker and float about;"[14]

There is also appreciable evidence that the fays have a distinctive gliding motion. Implicit in this is the possibility that they may be hovering above the surface of the ground, rather than being in contact and taking steps. It sounds from the reports as though they are not actually flying, nor are they walking.

The Reverend Robert Kirk, in *The Secret Commonwealth* described how the Highland *sith* (unlike the Manx little folk described earlier) "remove to other Lodgings at the Beginning of each Quarter of the Year ... Their chamælion-lyke Bodies swim in the Air near the Earth with Bag and Bagadge ...". Elsewhere, Kirk remarked how, with their bodies of "congealled Air," the *sith* folk are "some tymes caried aloft."[15]

---

11 Hogg, *Shepherd's Calendar*, 1829, vol.2, 215.

12 J. McDougall, *Waifs & Strays of Celtic Tradition*, vol.3, 'Craignish Tales,' 282 (note to page 95).

13 *County Folklore*, vol.3, 'Shetland and Orkney,' 22.

14 *Old Donald*, Menella Bute Smedley.

15 Kirk, *Secret Commonwealth*, chapters 1 & 2.

In the late eighteenth century, the Welsh Reverend Edmund Jones related how Edmund Daniel of Arail saw faeries at Cefn Bach: they were "leaping and striking the air" in an undulating motion. A late Victorian report from the Inner Hebrides reported something comparable. A man walking home at night heard a strange whistling sound, like a flock of plovers in flight, and then, turning towards the sound, he saw another man passing him on the road, but this figure wasn't solid like an ordinary body and seemed to float past. In another Highland case, one moonlit night two women were seen 'swimming' in the air, just above the ground. These latter descriptions are so individual and unique as to lend them considerable authenticity.[16]

Gliding does seem to be particularly characteristic of the northern Scottish faeries, at the very least: their dogs, the *cu sith,* have a gliding motion, as does the *glaistig,* and an early twentieth century Scottish folklorist was told by a Mrs Stewart about a moorland sighting of a slender woman in a gauzy green, rainbow-tinted, dress who glided ahead of her over the tops of the heather. On Orkney the king of the trows might be seen, gliding from farm yard to farm yard, casting a spell over the crops. A man abducted from his garden by the faeries at Breadalbane found himself gently skimming across the tops of the undisturbed corn in the field over the wall from his home.[17]

Lastly, a nineteenth century Yorkshire account described male and female faeries, of human adult size, early on summer mornings, in "rapid, confused motion." Faeries observed at Kington in Herefordshire were seen to be dancing above the ground. They "looked like children, leaping and frisking in the air." The Welsh *tylwyth teg* were said to dance on the tops

---

16 Jones, *The Appearance of Evil* no.59; Campbell & Hall, *Strange Things,* 267, no.38 & 268 no.41.

17 Campbell, *Superstitions of the Highlands and Islands,* 4; Campbell, *Popular Superstitions,* 141 & 160; Grant, *Myth, Tradition & Story from Western Argyllshire,* 1925, 29; *County Folklore,* vol.3, 21; L. Spence, *Fairy Tradition in Britain,* 65.

of rushes and heather, again suggestive of a light and floating motion. It need not be sedate though – the descriptions make clear that the faeries may be both active and swift.[18]

SILENT MOVEMENT

"In they swept with a rustling sound,
Like dead leaves blown together."[19]

Given that they frequently fly or float through the air, faery movement is particularly likely to be soundless, which may indeed explain some of the names given to the Highland *sith*. As many readers may well know, the Irish and Scottish Gaelic name for the faeries is *sidhe/ sith*. One of the derivations of this term is from the word for 'peace.' Translations of the name therefore give us 'the People of Peace,' the 'still folk' or 'the silently moving folk.' One interpretation of 'peace' is that it is a euphemistic name – an expression of hope as much as a description, a form of wish or charm that the fays will be peaceful in their conduct and leave us mortals in peace, just as use of the 'Good Neighbours' aspires to a state of amity between supernaturals and humans. Others have taken the term to be a simple physical description. For example, one author described how the faeries of the Scottish Lowlands move with "noiseless steps" as they steal silently around; in the Highlands, the *sith* folk are reported to glide or float soundlessly.[20]

Expert on Highland folklore, John Gregorson Campbell, believed that such an adjective was entirely appropriate in the circumstances:

---

18 Rev. M. Morris, *Yorkshire Folk-talk,* 1892, c.9; E. Leather, *Folklore of Herefordshire,* 43; Parry, *History of Kington,* 1845, 204; Rhys, *Celtic Folklore,* 83; *Y Geninen,* vol.13, 290; see too Wirt Sikes, *British Goblins,* 80.
19 *The Fairies' Cobbler,* Rosamond M. Watson.
20 E. Simpson, *Folklore of Lowland Scotland,* 1908, 91.

"Sound is a natural adjunct of the motions of men, and its entire absence is unearthly, unnatural, not human. The name *sith* without doubt refers to 'peace' or silence of Airy motion, as contrasted to the stir and noise accompanying the movements and actions of men. The German 'still folk' is a name of corresponding import ... They seem to glide or float along, rather than to walk."

Campbell compared the sound of the faeries' movement to a rustling noise, like that of a gust of wind, or a silk gown, or a sword drawn sharply through the air.[21]

The soundlessness of faery movement seems to be confirmed by an account collected by Welsh minister Edmund Jones. A girl of Trefethin parish told him how she once had come across some faeries dancing under a crab tree. Regularly after that, for a period of three or four years, she would meet with them to dance in a barn – either when she was going to or coming home from school. The girl reported that the most notable thing about these faeries was that she never heard their feet whilst she was dancing with them. In fact, she learned to take off her own shoes so as to make no noise, as it seemed to her that the sound of feet on the ground was displeasing to them.[22]

PURSUIT

The same man who told James Hogg about the faeries on Halloween also had another supernatural experience, when he saw a crowd of fays travelling up Glen Entertrony. At first, he thought they were neighbours returning from the fair and tried to catch up with them to get the latest news. Although they were only twenty paces ahead of him, and he was running, he was

---

21 Campbell, *Popular Superstitions*, 4.
22 Edmund Jones, *Relation*, 49.

never able to reach them – and all the time they seemed to him to be standing still in a circle.[23]

A little earlier we saw an account of a similar inability to catch up with a host of faeries from the Isle of Man. Strikingly, the Manx little folk maintained a very similar distance between themselves and their mortal pursuer. These examples of the faery power to stay continually ahead of pursuers puts me in mind of an incident from the *Mabinogion*. In the story of *Pwyll, Lord of Dyfed,* Pwyll is seated on top of a faery hill when he sees faery princess Rhiannon riding past. He tries to pursue her, but can never catch her up however hard he spurs his horse.

The *tylwyth teg* of Dyfed are certainly very hard to catch. If you see them on one peak whilst standing on another, there's no point trying to go to the second mountain top for a closer look – because you'll find they've moved to the mountain top where you started. This elusiveness was seen once in the parishes of Pencarreg and Caio when the local young men met for a game of football. They saw a large group of the faeries dancing a short distance away and decided to try to catch them, but the dancers instantly moved to another place. The young men followed, in response to which the little folk reappeared at the first place. When the youths tried instead to surround them, the dancers simply vanished. Glamour and rapid magical travel over large distances make it almost impossible to overtake them if they don't choose it.[24]

23 Hogg, *Shepherd's Calendar*, vol.2, 216.
24 Ceredig Davies, *Folklore*, 128 & 130; Sikes, *Goblins*, 78–79.

Faery Travel

Despite all of the foregoing, it seems that most of the time the faeries get around in very prosaic ways: walking on their own two feet, or on something else's four feet, or using vehicles of one type or another.

HORSE RIDING

It's pretty well known that the faes ride horses (just as the surrounding human population would have done in times past) and these animals are always described as being proportionate to their size. So, for example, when Scottish witch suspect Margaret Alexander met with the "King of Farie" at Calder, he "horst her" (put her on a horse) and rode with her to Lintoun Brig, where they both dismounted and had intercourse. If the faery folk are seen to be the size of children, they'll be mounted on ponies; if they're seen smaller, the steeds might only be as big as greyhounds.

Just like humans, too, the faeries will use their horses for all suitable activities: the communal groups known as the 'trooping faeries' go out on their annual 'rades' in processions of horses, but they'll also hunt on them, exactly as would human gentry and nobles. Faery horses are reputed to be very swift ("as fast as the wind") and to be highly prized, being richly caparisoned when they are taken out. There is some suggestion here of weightlessness in these activities, though. Describing the Nithsdale faeries, Cromek said that they rode steeds "whose hoof would not print the new ploughed land or dash the dew from the crop of a harebell" and that they never deviated from straight lines in their travels, going straight through hedges and across corn fields to their destinations without leaving a trace on the crops.

Indeed, the explanation for these observations seems to be that faery horses aren't earthbound, as ours are – their steeds can float, just as their riders can. For example, at Aberpergwm in Wales the *tylwyth teg* were seen riding in the air on little mounts. Sometimes humans will ride alongside the faeries and, in such cases, it seems that the faeries' glamour somehow transfers itself to their mortal companions. A man from the Glencoe area went out to feasts and weddings with the faeries for a whole year. He accompanied them mounted on his own horse, but found that it would fly alongside them on their journeys. Lastly, we know of a Perthshire man, who was travelling back from Kenmore market to his home at the other end of Loch Tay. About half way along the shore, he heard music coming from a *sithean* at Lawers. He joined a faery celebration and had a good time there; to complete his journey he was given a white horse that flew through the air like lightening.[1]

Needless to say, it's often easier for riders to make use of someone else's animals – that way you don't have to stable, feed or generally care for them – and it's widely known that faeries do just this, taking horses from farmer's stables at night and riding them until they're worn out. This process is frequently accompanied by the knotting of the horses' manes and tails, at least some of which is done ostensibly to provide the diminutive riders with reins and stirrups. These are necessary not just because the faery horsemen are often so much tinier than their mounts, but because they like to drive the horses at frenetic pace across the fields and moors. These exertions leave the commandeered steeds exhausted, frothing at the mouth and covered in a foam of sweat, much to the dismay of their human owners.[2]

---

1 T. Crofton Croker, *Fairy Legends & Traditions*, Part 3, 224; B. Fairweather, *Folklore of Glencoe & Northern Lorn*, 1974, 2; J. Macdiarmid, 'Fragments of Breadalbane Folklore,' *Transactions of the Gaelic Society of Inverness*, vol.26, 1905, 37.

2 See, for example, the discussion in my *British Pixies*.

On Jersey the faeries will also ride horses left out in their pastures at night. They can be heard laughing and galloping in the dark and they will invariably choose the fattest and best conditioned steed. The East Anglian faeries prefer young horses – but still leave them covered in foam in their stables in the morning.[3]

OTHER MOUNTS

So far, so familiar, but it doesn't stop there. If horses aren't available, other four-legged beasts will do. On the Isle of Anglesey, it was reported that the local *tylwyth teg* rode donkeys or (to be exact) they gave a mortal man one to ride when he travelled with them. This might, conceivably, have been some sort of joke or put-down on their part: they got well-bred steeds and he got a bad-tempered ass. Another mortal in the same party, who seems to have insulted the fair folk by not eating their food, was made to ride a calf for the same journey.[4]

In fact, the faeries will ride any other available quadrupeds if no equines are available. It's said in Nithsdale in Scotland that they will ride cats (albeit turned into horses for the night) whilst in Ross-shire in the far north of the country cows would be ridden. Like horses, they may be found the following morning hot and distressed, a condition called *na marcaich* (the riders). The same is the case in Suffolk – and the remedy is the same as with horses. Any calf found very hot in its byre would have a holed flint hung over its back at a level to brush off any faery trying to ride it. On Orkney and Shetland, too, the trows ride the farmers' cows. It was recorded as late as 1970 that if, when cattle are put out to pasture in the spring, one of them is then found weak, collapsed

---

3   J. L'Amy, *Jersey Folklore,* 1927, 28; C. Partridge, 'Fairies in East Anglia,' *East Anglia Notes & Queries,* vol.10, 1903, 242.

4   W. Cobb, 'Anglesey Folklore,' *Y Cymmrodor,* vol.7, 1886, 115.

and frothing at the mouth, it will be because the trows have been riding the beast.[5]

Cats and cows at least have four legs, but we know that even two legged victims will do. According to the sixteenth century Scots poem, *Montgomerie's Flyting of Polwarth,* some of the Scottish elves were known to ride other two-legged creatures: *"Sum saidlit ane scho aip all grathit into green"* (some saddled a she-ape, all clad in green). What's more, there are reports from around the Britain Isles of unfortunate human victims being saddled and mounted to act as steeds for faeries overnight.

The use of human steeds at night (which will involve tying their hair in 'elf-locks') was especially prevalent on the Isle of Man but was also known on the Isle of Arran. The victims feel no weight on their backs during the experience, but they become tired for loss of sleep and thin and weak from their exertions. From Arran, we hear of a woman who suddenly fell ill and became very tired and sleepy. Her family suspected that she was suffering from no ordinary fatigue and they watched her at night. They discovered that the faeries were coming when the household was asleep and were turning her into a horse, which they then used for their carting. A search of the garden the next morning uncovered a hidden harness, which helped break the spell cast upon her. Wearing a flower or herb to scare off the faeries should be enough to prevent this version of the 'nightmare' (see earlier).[6]

Also from Scotland, we have the confession of suspected witch Isobel Gowdie that she had gone out with the faery host, the *sluagh,* to shoot elf-bolts at hapless humans. Of these random victims she said:

> "we may shoot them dead at owr pleasour. Any that ar shot be us, their sowell will goe to Hevin, bot ther bodies remain with us, and will flie as horsis to us, as small as strawes."[7]

5 W. Wilson, *Folklore of Uppermost Nithsdale,* 1904, 99; E. Porter, *Folklore of East Anglia,* 1974, 78; *Tobar an Dulchais,* 28/9/1970.

6 Roeder, *Manx Folk Tales,* 11–12; MacKenzie, *Book of Arran,* 1914, 267.

7 Pitcairn, *Ancient Criminal Trials,* vol.3, part 2, 602.

Humans, in fact, often act as beasts of burden as well as being mounts for the faes. A widow from Athol in Perthshire asked the local wise man, Alasdair Callum, what had become of her vanished husband. She was told that he was with the faeries of Slevach Cairn, put to work as a baggage horse with a twisted willow withy in his mouth.[8]

Modern fantasy art often shows faes riding birds and other wildlife. Pretty as these images are, and despite the fact that we are attracted to them because they emphasise the unity of the faeries with their environment, there is not very much traditional support for the idea. As we've just seen, we hear of the elves riding apes, but they must be few and far between in any part of Britain; it's also reported that the Highland hag, the *cailleach bheur,* and her followers ride on wolves and swine. The Gyre Carling, another name for the faery queen in Fife, was also said to ride a pig: in one poem she "schup her on ane sow and is her gaitis gane" (she settled herself on a sow and went her ways). Nevertheless, making use of more common mammals and fowls is not reported.[9]

8 Robertson, 'Folklore from the West of Ross-shire,' *Transactions of the Gaelic Society of Inverness,* vol.26, 1905, 286; MacKenzie, *The Book of Arran,* 1914, 267; Campbell, *Superstitions,* 94.
9 For details of the gyre carlin, see my *Who's Who in Faeryland.*

Transport

As well as walking and riding, the faeries will, exactly like humans, use various sorts of conveyance whenever that is necessary or convenient.

COACHES

The faes are known to have coaches and carriages. For example, at Llyn Idwal on the Llanllechid mountain neat Bethesda, a beautiful carriage drawn by six horses was seen dashing along the hillside and then into the lake itself. At Cwm Mabws, near Llanrhystyd, the *tylwyth teg* are said to live in the caves of Craig Rhydderch. They have often been seen travelling along the cwm itself with horses and carriages – for example, in 1860 two separate witnesses at different points on the valley road encountered the same faery coach. Meanwhile, in Devon, a coach of bones has been seen travelling between Okehampton and Fitzford House.[1]

A vivid description was given by Reginald Scot in his *Discoverie of Witchcraft* of abductions by the flying faery host:

> "many such have been taken away by the said spirits for a fortnight or a month together, being carried with them in chariots through the air, over hills and dales, rocks and precipices, and passing over many countries and nations in the silence of the night, bereaved of their sense and commonly of their members to boot."[2]

---

1 E. Owen, 'Folklore, Superstitions & What Not,' *Montgomeryshire Collections,* vol.15, 1882, 138; J. Ceredig Davies, *Folklore of West & Mid Wales,* 1911, 129; E. Tozer. *Devonshire & Other Original Poems,* 1873, 90.
2 Scot, *Discoverie of Witchcraft,* 1584, Book III, c.IV.

Scot's introduction of the flying 'chariots' is a unique and fascinating feature but his depiction of the effect of these prolonged aerial abductions certainly fits very well with the descriptions given earlier of the experience of flying with the *sluagh*. Scot's addition of a vehicle is not found elsewhere but is not wholly improbable. It should be added that 'chariot' – like the archaic usage of 'car' – simply denotes some sort of wheeled conveyance of some kind; it doesn't imply that the faeries were careering around in some Roman style military vehicle.

CARTS & WAGONS

We hear of faeries moving house. When they do so, they tend to move in a conventional human manner, with horses pulling carts. In one sighting from Sutherland during the late 1860s the witness saw three carts laden with furniture and other household possessions being dragged by hand over the moorland where there was no road and in a direction in which no human habitation lay. When the church bells drove the pixies out of their home at Withypool on Exmoor, they borrowed a local farmer's horse and cart to make the move (and returned the horses looking years younger). Such equipment might in fact be needed much more regularly. On Guernsey the Garis family was visited nightly by their faery neighbours, asking for the loan of their farm cart until dawn. This regular inconvenience was offset by the fact that faeries always promised to return the wagon in perfect condition, with any damage to the woodwork repaired with silver.[3]

BOATS

To travel upon water, the faeries will naturally use boats (as we heard earlier, the *sluagh* certainly have no difficulty flying above

---

3   R. Tongue, *Somerset Folklore*, 117; E. MacCulloch, *Guernsey Folklore*, 1903, 212.

the waves). The fishing fleets of the little folk have been a well-known sight off the Isle of Man and in North East Scotland. On Man, they have been seen building boats at Perwick and their pleasure craft have been encountered out at sea too.[4]

As ever, if the faeries lack their own craft, they will simply take someone else's. On Shetland the trows are known to do this, a liberty compounded by the fact that they never tie up the boats when they'd finished with them. The Guernsey faes are reported to have magical boats which have the property of mysteriously getting smaller as they near land (a circumstance which might also suggest that the often-reported diminutive stature of faeries is something adopted by them whenever they're in our vicinity – for some reason that's unknown to us).[5]

MECHANISED TRANSPORT

Much of what has been described so far suggests that the faeries are stuck in a pre-modern, unmechanised world – something that is often our view of them. We like to romanticise their pre-industrial, rural aspects, whereas the evidence indicates that they move with the times just as much as their human neighbours do. For instance, they are craftspeople – they are metal workers, builders, spinners and weavers – but faery industry is known as well – dyeing and milling, for example.[6] More pertinently, contemporary reports indicate that they will use cars, buses and aeroplanes to get around. Humans no longer *need* to employ horse power, although they will use them for special occasions and special purposes; the same would seem to be true of the

---

4 J. Napier, *Folklore or Superstitions*, 1879, 65; Gill, *Second Manx Scrapbook*, 1932, c.6; *Yn Lioar Manninagh,* vol.3, 1899, 482 & vol.4, 154–161; *Manx Notes and Queries*, 1904, 131 & 158; Morrison, *Manx Fairy Tales*, 1911, 'Little footprints'; Roeder, *Manx Folk Tales,* 'Fairies of Sea & Shore'.

5 *Tobar an Dulchais,* 22/9/1970; M. de Garis, *Folklore of Guernsey*, 1975, 146.

6 For faery industry see my *How Things Work in Faery*.

British faery. The mystery, with all of this, is why they bother with any sort of conveyance at all. Considering what we already know about the faeries' abilities to move around, use of either horsepower or the internal combustion engine seems entirely unnecessary. Perhaps novelty is the only explanation for this baffling attraction.[7]

Most surprisingly, this fascination with modern transport seems to include the use of railways. Given the faeries' reported tendency to flee the noise and clamour of the human world, whether that is church bells or the noise of a factories, quarries and mills, it seems unlikely that they would take to locomotives of any description. Accordingly, describing the Isle of Man for his *Practical Guide* of 1874, Henry Irwin Jenkinson recognised that belief in the Manx faeries was dying out amongst the islanders under the assault of education and the rationalism of the younger generation. Worse still, he wrote:

> "Now there are railways and the island is overrun with tourists every summer, the last haunts of the good people will be invaded and they will have to move elsewhere."[8]

The fear of modern mechanised transport expelling Britain's supernatural residents had in fact been expressed as early as the 1840s, when a correspondent of *Notes and Queries* had worried that railway engines would drive faeries far away from 'Merry England.'[9]

Yet, we also have this bizarre story from Man: in the south of the island, a person reported sighting faeries operating a railway – over two decades before the first track had even been laid on Man, which happened as late as 1873:

---

7 See for example Marjorie Johnson, *Seeing Fairies*, 2014, 35, 55, 64 & 251 or *Fairy Census*, numbers 29, 38 & 177
8 Henry Jenkinson, *Practical Guide to the Isle of Man,* 75.
9 *Notes & Queries*, vol.9, 1860, 259.

"There was a man from Santon told me last night that an uncle of his used to see the fairies very often, while he was alive, and knew a great deal about them. He was often telling the people about the railway line, more than twenty years before anyone thought about it. He was seeing the fairies very often practising on it in the moonlight, and he could point out where the line was to be, as he was seeing fairy trains going along so often ... The man said the railway line was made on the very spot he told them, more than twenty years before it was proposed."[10]

In isolation, this story seems to make no sense at all. However, the same man went on to say that his uncle was able to predict how good the fishing season would be according to the types of faery he saw in and around his home. Now, this link between seeing faeries and predicting the future is common, both on Man and elsewhere. In this context, although the apparition was a long time in advance of the event portrayed, it was completely not out of the ordinary for faery behaviour.

Further, the involvement of the fays with mechanical transport is a trend that has begun to emerge in more recent reports of sightings. Obviously, faeries need neither planes, nor trains, nor automobiles to be able to fly or to travel around at speed, but they seem to have some partiality to showing themselves to us with our own modern technology. Most famous is the 'Wollaton incident' in Nottingham in 1979 when a number of little men were seen driving around a park in hovering cars. Unique as it is in many respects, the sighting is not alone. A small girl and her sisters in Cornwall in the 1940s were woken one night by a buzzing sound. Looking out of their bedroom window, they saw a small gnome-like man driving a tiny red car in circles. In 1929 two children under ten living in Hertford witnessed a faery flying a biplane over their garden.[11]

10   Gill, *Second Manx Scrapbook*, c.3.
11   Simon Young (ed), *The Wollaton Gnomes*, 2022; Janet Bord, *Fairies*, 73–76.

As well as motor vehicles, there appears to be a developing faery fascination with machinery in all its forms. Marjorie Johnson recorded cases of faeries drawn to type-writers and sewing machines, as well as an incident when some 'leprechauns' diagnosed a fault in a bus engine. Faeries have also been seen by train passengers, on the platform or keeping pace with the train itself, and by those in cars, when again the fays fly alongside the vehicle.[12]

All this suggests that, just as faery magic can be fascinating for us, the wonder of humans' technical marvels may be just as intriguing for them.

SUMMARY

Faery motion is a subject that seems to be full of complexity and variation. Their tendency to kidnap and carry off humans might indicate that they generally employ magical powers to get around and to transport loads, animate or inanimate. However, their very well-established habit of using a range of forms of transport plainly goes against such ideas. Then again, I can't think of a case in which a human abductee was ever bundled into a carriage or thrown across a horse and carried off by that means.

It's worth reflecting, too, upon the implications of what we've read in this Part for the whole issue of faery pastimes discussed in Part Three. Most of the sports described are enjoyed by humans as well and our natural tendency is to imagine the faery equivalents being played in exactly the same, with boots (or hooves) firmly in contact with the muddy playing field or race course, and all the physical aspects that follow from that. However, we read earlier about a Cornish hurling match that seemed to disappear over a cliff, as well as Irish examples which appear to have been played over the sea. These examples strongly suggest the faeries were floating and gliding at speed.

---

12 *Seeing Fairies*, 101 & 322; *Census* numbers 169 & 456 and 105 & 213.

PART FIVE

Faeries & Witches' Familiars

There is a well-established conventional idea of the faeries' appearance. I shall cite two recent books to illustrate this. Firstly, in 2007 an authority on Anglo Saxon elves summarised them as "corporeal, anthropomorphic beings, mirroring the human in-groups who believe in them." In 2018, the faeries were defined as being "magical, living, resident humanoids." I wouldn't take fundamental issue with either of these statements, and I have adopted them myself in most of my writing; nonetheless, there is some evidence to indicate that earlier generations entertained a much broader conception of what constituted a faery.[1]

I have already, in this book, referred several times to the evidence of sixteenth and seventeenth century trials of Scottish individuals suspected of witchcraft and sorcery. These defendants were mentioned because they often claimed to have contact with faeries, visiting them under their hills and deriving from them various skills, such as predicting the future and treating various ailments. In these Scottish cases, there was direct, personal contact with the 'Good Wights' and they were encountered as people very similar to the defendants themselves – to the extent, even, that sexual contact sometimes took place.

From the mid-sixteenth century onwards, a similar 'witch scare' took place in England, leading to comparable accusations, arrests, interrogations and executions of individuals (as in Scotland, mainly women) whose conduct had given rise to suspicions of sorcery. What's notable about the English cases, though, is the fact that references to contact with the faeries are

---

1   A. Hall, *Elves in Anglo-Saxon England,* 2007, 68; S. Young & C. Houlbrook, *Magical Folk,* 2018, 12. See, too, my own *Faery Lifecycle,* 2021.

largely absent. Instead, there was the "peculiarly English notion" that witches were aided by (and frequently identified by) their 'familiars,' creatures provided by the devil to perform magical services on their behalf. British folklore authority Ronald Hutton has characterised England as the "stronghold of the tradition" of familiars, beings that acted as "agents and instigators of witchcraft, whose intentions and actions were almost wholly malevolent." He observed too, that the idea emerged in the Tudor period.[2]

2 K. Thomas, *Religion & The Decline of Magic,* 1978, 530' Hutton, *The Witch,* 2017, 262 & 272.

Faeries & Imps

As several scholars have remarked, before about 1560 in England there was no record of any popular belief in the beings that came to be called familiars or 'imps.' That being the case, as one author has observed, "It is hardly credible that imps were a distinct category of supernatural being in folklore whose existence was simply never recorded until the advent of the trials for witchcraft, and it is much more likely that they were an outgrowth, in some way, of fairylore." In other words, imps and familiars were one manifestation of faeries that was experienced in England – and one that has now largely been forgotten.[1]

We should start with a short discussion of the terminology employed. Firstly, we should define 'familiar' as it was understood at the time. As well as two sober texts on the administration of local justice, barrister Michael Dalton (1564–1644) wrote *The Discoverie of Witches* in 1613. He explained how witches:

> "ordinarily have a familiar or spirit, which appeareth unto them; sometimes in one shape, sometimes in another, as in the shape of a man, woman, boy, dog, cat, foal, fowl, hare, rat, toad etc. And to these their spirits they give names and they meet together to christen them (as they speak). Their sayd Familiar hath some big or little teat upon their body, and in some secret place, where he sucketh them. And besides their sucking, the Devil leaveth other marks upon their body, sometimes like a blew spot, or red spot, like a flea-biting; sometimes the flesh sunk in and hollow (all which for a time may be covered, yea taken away, but will

---

1 F. Young, *Suffolk Fairylore,* 2019, 68; E. Wilby, *Cunning Folk & Familiar Spirits,* 2005, 50 and 'The Witch's Familiar and the Fairy in Early Modern England and Scotland,* Folklore,* vol.111, 2000, 283–305; D. Purkiss, *Troublesome Things,* 2001, 153; Thomas, *Religion & The Decline of Magic,* 727.

come again, to their old form.) And these the Devils marks be insensible, and being pricked will not bleed, and be often in their secretest parts, and therefore require diligent and careful search."

Hence, Dalton advised, the main way to expose a person as a witch was to find that s/he had a familiar, which the suspect addressed by name and fed secretly, typically by suckling or by giving them their own blood. Readers may appreciate that this feeding of the imp might well find parallels in the habit of giving bread, cream and suchlike to faeries, most especially the domestic brownies and hobs. At the same time, of course, many entirely innocent individuals might have been caught by Dalton's test merely because they had in their home a named pet that they fed.

Secondly, during the early modern period, familiars went by a variety of terms. The most common is the word 'imp,' 'impet' or 'impling.'This derives from a Latin word meaning a tree graft and, in this sense (but perhaps with an extra layer of meaning already present) it's used in the Middle English poem *Sir Orfeo*, in which the knight's wife is abducted by the faery king when she is asleep under a *"fair ympe-tre."* The word subsequently acquired other meanings, such as 'offshoot' and 'offspring,' thereby coming to signify a child and a small demon. Another word that will be often encountered is 'puckrel,' as in George Gifford's *Dialogue on Witches*, published in 1683, which recounted how one old woman, suspected of being a witch, "had three or foure imps, some call them puckrels, one like a gray catte, an other like a weasell, an other like a mouse."[2]

A further term occasionally employed is 'hag.' According to a pamphlet called *The Scotish Dove*, witches at Bury St Edmunds in 1645 sent out their 'hags' (or imps) to help the Royalist army. As

---

2 Scott, 'The Devil & His Imps,' *Transactions of the American Philological Association*, vol. 26, 1895, 110; Gifford, *Dialogue*, 3.

well as an attempt to link King Charles with the devil, we here see another supernatural entity that has been caught up within the witch craze. Further terms employed from time to time include angel, little master, fury, maumet and nigget. It's worth adding as well that the witches themselves often named their imps, and that the names chosen are ones also used for faeries and for quite a few of the other supernatural beings we've discussed – such as Robin, Jack, Tom, Dick, Hob, Jill, Blue Cap, Jenny and Red Cap. This may simply indicate a wish to personalise and defuse something frightening, or it might imply some deeper, shared origin.[3]

There are a couple of recorded cases which make the link between faeries and witches' imps pretty clear. Firstly, in August 1566, a Dorset man called John Walsh was examined by magistrates on charges of sorcery. He described contacts with the "feries," whom he met at midday or midnight on local hills. He would also light candles inside circles to "raise the familiar spirit – of whom he would then ask for anything stolen and where the stolen thing was left, and thereby did know, and also by the Feries he knoweth who be bewitched." Walsh's familiar appeared to him as a black dove, a brindled dog or as a man with cloven feet and would help him find stolen horses and "doo any thing at his commaundement, in going anye arrant [errand]" – although it first required that candles were lit and that frankincense and St John's wort were burned. Although the male figure sounds like a demon, all Walsh's other statements seem to treat the familiar spirit and the "fery" as being identical.[4]

Secondly, in March 1618, Joan Willimott, from Goadby in Leicestershire, was examined as a witch. She claimed to have received a spirit named Pretty from a man called William Berry, whom "she served three yeares." Berry is said to have asked Joan "to open her mouth, and hee would blow into her a Fairy which

---

3 M. Gaskill, *Witchfinders*, 2005, 166; P. Hughes, *Witchcraft*, 1970, 154.
4 *The Examination of John Walsh Before Master Thomas Williams*, Aug. 1566.

should doe her good; and that shee opened her mouth, and he did blow into her mouth." After this, the spirit emerged from Joan's mouth and stood before her on the ground "in the shape and form of a woman." Pretty acted as a consultant to Willimott, meeting with her weekly to tell her who in the neighbourhood had been "stricken or fore-spoken" (that is, cursed or bewitched). Joan would then go to those people and cure them with prayers. Although she was explicit that Pretty was a benign fairy (and not a demoniac familiar) and that she never hurt anyone, nevertheless, Pretty still "did aske of her her Soule, which shee then promised unto it."

Willimott was tried with several other female accomplices, all of whom had their own familiars, but these were all animals – two cats, a rat, an owl, a mouse, a mole and a dog. These creatures are typical of the imps that witch suspects were accused of associating with and, if we accept that the idea of familiars must have derived from an earlier concept of faery helpers, it opens up to us a whole new perspective on faery appearance and identity. We are used to the idea that they can shape shift into a variety of forms (other than the humanoid) but the possibility that they will permanently (or, at least, mainly) assume animal shapes is a departure from current conventional understanding.

Before examining this question in detail, we'll consider one further story. With Willimot and Walsh, we are confronted with faeries who behave like familiars. In the traditional tale of Tom Tit Tot, we encounter an imp whom it is conventional to accept as a faery. *Tom Tit Tot* is one of several English language versions of the German fairy story *Rumpelstiltskin*. The best-known version was recorded in Suffolk dialect by Edward Clodd.[5]

The tale involves a young woman given an impossible task (spinning) who is offered help by a supernatural being, on condition that she guess his name or become his forever. Tom

---

5   See K. Briggs, *Dictionary of Fairies*, 404–409, for Clodd's text; see my *Who's Who in Faery* for a consideration of the British versions of this theme.

Tit Tot is described as a "little black thing with a long tail." He is also repeatedly termed an "impet." Probably, most readers would classify Tom Tit Tot as a 'goblin.' His status is, plainly, ambiguous and it is probably mainly due to our habit of treating the Grimm Brothers' *Rumpelstiltskin* and similar tales as 'fairy stories' that we unhesitatingly regard Tom as faery rather than demon. Consider, by contrast, the Cornish version of the story, which was recorded by Robert Hunt. *Duffy and the Devil* is included in his collection of *Popular Romances of the West of England* in the section on 'Demons and Spectres' and features a "queer looking little man" dressed in black who undertakes to do the required knitting and spinning for the heroine, subject to the usual conditions. Throughout the story he is referred to as a "devil," a Cornish cousin to Beelzebub or Lucifer. He disappears with fire and smoke when his real name, Terrytop, is revealed. Terrytop is much more definitely demonic than Tom Tit Tot, whereas the malign characters in the stories of Welsh *Trwtyn-Tratyn* and *Peerifool*, from Orkney, are just as evidently faeries: in the latter case, he is one of the *Peerie Folk*, the 'little people.' These examples underline for us how uncertain and shifting so many of our labels may be.

The Form of Familiars

The records of English witch trials reveal that imps could appear in a wide range of forms – mammals, birds, insects, crustacea and others.[1] Rare instances include snails, a crab and a spider whilst about seven per cent of cases were insects, such as flies, bees, butterflies, a wasp, a 'dor' (a large beetle such as a cockchafer) and a 'miller' (a large white moth). A little under a fifth of imps took bird form, ranging from domesticated chickens and turkeys to doves and a crow.

As a rule, as may already be seen, familiars were regarded as small – if not tiny; hence Goody Smith of Bramford, near Ipswich, kept her imps in bag concealed under her skirt. Not only were they safely hidden there, but the implication is that that there was some sort of intimate contact too. The occasional dog of medium size or less seems to have been as large as most familiars came. The only exception to this is an instance from Laindon in Essex where a parson (who was also, oddly, a wizard) kept three imps. They were once seen by a domestic servant in a room, standing against the legs of a table and as high as the top of the table. This indicates that they may have been about a metre tall. Their form is not described but, if it was humanoid, we would in any other context conclude that she had seen some faeries.[2]

A further demonstration of the generally small size of imps comes from another sighting of one of the same parson's imps at Laindon. On this second occasion, the creature was seen walking across the tips of nettles, and was reportedly so light that the plants didn't even bend under its weight. Although the incident doesn't sound especially awful, the witness was so terrified that he gave up his job at the farm where the parson lived. As described earlier, accounts of the Welsh faeries have described

1   G. Parrinder, *Witchcraft*, 1958, 42–43.
2   C. Craven Mason, *Essex – Its Forest, Folk & Folklore*, 1928, 116.

them walking on the tips of rushes and heather in an identical manner.[3]

Toads, which are very regularly associated with witches, were mentioned in about a tenth of cases. In fact, it seems that they were employed often enough by witches in Cambridgeshire that 'tudding' (apparently derived from 'toad') became a dialect word for 'bewitching.' Toads were believed to be poisonous, which was one reason for keeping them. Dorset cunning man John Walsh described how they were employed as imps:

> "And as touching the using of the Todes, the which he sayth have several names: som they cal great Browning, or little Brownyng, or Bonne, great Tom Twite, or litle Tom Twite, with other like names: Which Todes being called ... they commaunde the Tode to hurt such a man or woman as he would have hurted. Whereto if he swell, he will goo wher he is apointed, either to the deiry, brewhouse, or to the dry kill of malt, or to the Cattel in the field, to the stable, to the shepefold, or to any other like places, and so returne agayne to his place ... mens goods & Cattels be hurt by the Todes, in commaunding and using them, as aforesaid, as he sayth. And if the Tode called forth, as afore said, do not swell, then will the Witch that useth them cal forth an other to do the act ..."[4]

Nearly two-thirds of the imps were mammals, such as 'moldewarps' (moles), a ferret, a weasel and polecats, dogs, bats, a pig, a lamb and rabbits. Mice (and a few rats) made up about a fifth of the familiars reported. Some shapeshifting by the creatures was apparently possible. We have heard the Laindon

---

3 S. Cooper, *A Sussex Book of Witch Legends,* 89; Westwood & Simpson, *Lore of the Land,* 263; Craven Mason, *Essex: Its Forest, Folk & Folklore,* 117.

4 E. Porter, *Cambridgeshire Customs & Folklore,* 2020, 50 & 189, fn.1; *The examination of John Walsh of Dorsetshere, touching Witchcraft and Sorcerie,* 1566.

imps described as being as tall as children; another time one looked like a black cat and on a further occasion like a mole.[5]

Bats are mentioned in about ten cases – less than we might expect today, given their modern vampiric associations. One case, from Loddon in Norfolk, is especially interesting, though. It concerns an old woman and her daughter, Mary. The mother was a witch who kept two imps. These described as being "a right little sort of fairy, like a person, right enough, but with wings like a bat." They could assume any size they chose, but tended to stay small so they could be kept in a box. The witch kept them as they would answer any questions she wished to pose to them; additionally, women who themselves wanted to become witches would come to her and the imps would be released to crawl on them and bite their breasts. There is clearly something perversely sexual about this (rather like the imps get in a bag by the thighs), and the macabre erotic imagery must elicits thoughts of the troubled nightmares discussed in Part Two, but it evokes other associations as well. Firstly, the idea of suckling and giving the imps blood are combined; secondly, it may suggest to us those faery beings that subsist upon human blood. A variety of 'vampire' faeries are encountered across the British Isles. In both Scotland and the Isle of Man, if no water was left out at night in homes for any faery visitors, they might quench their thirsts by taking the sleeping humans' blood. In Cromarty, in the Highlands, it was believed that a 'Lady in Green' carried her child from cottage to cottage at night, bathing it in the blood of the youngest inhabitant found in each. There are similar Highland tales of bird-like green women who crack bones and drink blood; finally, there are tales from Skye and Lochaber of humans staying overnight in shielings who are visited by mysterious females and drained of their blood.[6]

---

5   Craven Mason, *Essex: Its Forest, Folk & Folklore,* 116.
6   M.H. James, *Bogie Tales of East Anglia,* 1891, 25; Westwood & Simpson, *Lore of the Land,* 507; Spence, *The Fairy Tradition in Britain* chapter 14, 268–269; H. Miller, *Scenes and Legends of the North of Scotland,* 1835, 15.

Surprisingly, perhaps, cats and kittens (the archetypal witch familiar, for many people today) accounted for only about a tenth of cases. Still, the possibility that faeries might very well appear in cat form may explain the experience of Margaret Alexander of Livingston, who was tried for witchcraft in March 1647. She confessed that she had been "mightily troubled in her house at night with a rumbling and [the] many kats [that] resorted there." On one occasion, in about 1600, a number of these "kats" had appeared to her at Calder Watergate in the town; they had been the size of sheep and had then turned into men and women, many of whom she knew to be dead. These people carried her a distance of sixteen miles and ate and drank with her before returning her home – yet "she was not the better for the food." Many aspects of this case suggest that Margaret encountered some faery folk: the rapid travel, the insubstantial food, the presence of those apparently dead. Their initial manifestation as oversized felines might have seemed at odds with this conclusion, until we consider the descriptions of witches' imps.[7]

The evidence on witches' animal familiars tends to surprise and to puzzle because it is not what we anticipate. Much more predictable to us are the six familiars recorded that looked like children: faeries are widely described as appearing like small people or infants, so these imps do not strike us as in the least out of the ordinary. Margaret Moore of Ely, tried in 1647, confessed that one evening the spirits of her dead children had spoken to her and persuaded her into making a pact with the devil so as to save her last surviving child from death. On another occasion, a spirit had appeared to her as a naked child and had sucked her blood. This incident could easily be understood as some kind of bargain with Faery to avert a further child abduction. Contact with abducted individuals (who may appear to have died) is not at all uncommon, although usually it is adults (typically

---

7 A. Macdonald, 'A Witchcraft Case of 1647,' *Scots Law Times*, April 10th 1937, 77–78.

kidnapped females) that get in touch with the mortal family they have left behind. There is, however, the example of Malekin, who appeared at Dagworth manor in Suffolk in the late twelfth century. She was a local girl who had been stolen by the faeries from her mother when they were out in the fields one day. She spoke regularly to the inhabitants of the manor house, explaining that she would be able to return to her family after seven years with the faeries. It might be added, though, that 'malkin' was used as a name for the devil.[8]

Lastly, Aubrey Grinset of Dunwich on the Suffolk coast was tried as a witch in 1667. Her imp was a "Pretty handsome Young Man" who regularly appeared to her – sometimes as a dark grey kitten. Likewise, in March 1646, Elizabeth Weed of Great Catworth in Huntingdonshire confessed to having three imps, two in animal shape and one a young man who slept with her. These descriptions are clearly highly suggestive of the incubi discussed in Part Two.

To summarise the evidence so far, there are numerous parallels to be found between imps and faeries, all of which tend to confirm the proposal that witches' familiars are, indeed, a form of faery being. As we shall see in more detail, these imps were not wholly evil and demonic. They could do good as well as bad and, as such, very closely resemble the typical British with its rather ambivalent character.

---

8 Porter, *Folklore of East Anglia,* 140; for Dagworth, see, for example, Francis Young, *Suffolk Fairylore,* c.2 & Appendix 2; Scott, 'The Devil & His Imps,' *Transactions of the American Philological Association,* vol. 26, 1895, 118.

Shapeshifting Faeries

Many of the examples of imps just given challenge our preconceptions of faeries quite severely. However, I think this is only because we tend to overlook the folklore evidence as a whole and to dismiss reports of less conventional forms as aberrations or exceptions when they may not, in fact, be so. On consulting the folklore record, we find quite a significant number of examples of faeries adopting, more or less continuously, the form of animals that we have already seen might be found as witches' imps.

The arch shapeshifter in Faery is Robin Goodfellow or Puck. According to the *Ballad of Robin Goodfellow*, he can transform into a variety of different people, inanimate objects and, also, appears as a fox, a hare, an owl, a frog, a horse, a crow, a hog and a hound. Interestingly, in Thomas Shadwell's play, *The Lancashire Witches,* the character Puck Hairy is described as "an imp like a black shock" – a 'shock' or 'shug' being a supernatural beast or bogie taking the form of a black dog or similar animal. Equally, when George Gascoigne listed types of faery-being in his play *The Buggbears,* he enumerated "puckes, puckerels … and Robin Goodfellow." As we have already seen, both 'imp' and puckrel' may denote a familiar, so that these statements may have more significance than we might appreciate at first reading.[1]

We saw in the previous Part how the flying faery host may be mistaken for birds; some actually take on avian form. Cornish pixies can metamorphose into a variety of small birds, such as redbreasts, yellow-hammers and wag-tails. The pixies can also take on goat form (so as to entice away the best milkers from

---

1 Shadwell, *Lancashire Witches,* 1682, Act 3; Gascoigne, *Buggbears,* 1565, Act III, line 58; on the black dogs and shugs, see my *Beyond Faery,* 2020. On Puck see my *Who's Who in Faery,* 2022.

human flocks). The faeries on Guernsey may appear at night as goats with fiery eyes. In an account from Sutherland, a man resting on a faery knoll saw what he thought was a flock of goats approaching; as they got nearer, though, he realised that they were in fact little people dressed in many different colours. The Welsh fairies, the *tylwyth teg*, are able to appear as goats as well, although, in fact, they can shape-shift into a variety of animal forms, including dogs, cats and foxes.[2]

The pixies also seem to have distinct connections with moths. Folklorist Robert Hunt recorded in his *Popular Romances of the West of England* how "Mr Thoms has noticed that in Cornwall 'the moths which some regard as departed souls, others as fairies, are called *Pisgies*.'" Hunt commented upon this by suggesting that it was "somewhat too generally expressed; the belief respecting the moth, so far as I know, is confined to one or two varieties only." Still, Hunt went on to note that, around Polperro, the weasel is called the *fairy* and he concluded that all of this was "evidence of some sort of metempsychosis amongst the elf family. Moths, ants, and weasels – it would seem – are the forms taken by those wandering spirits." This statement was supported by Walter Evans Wentz, who was told in Penzance that miners believed white moths to be spirits.[3]

The Mr Thoms mentioned by Robert Hunt had written about 'The Folklore of Shakespeare' in *The Athenaeum* in 1847. In this article he also recorded that in the Truro area of mid-Cornwall moths and pixies were thought to be identical. What's more, at St Nun's Well near Looe, on the south coast of the Cornish peninsula, there is a tradition of leaving a bent pin as an offering. If a person neglects to do this, they will be followed home by a

---

2 M. de Garis, *Folklore of Guernsey*, 1975, 154; *www.tobarandualchais.co.uk*, July 1960; *Wrexham & Denbighshire Advertiser*, April 20th 1878, 7: 'Welsh Fairy Mythology.'
3 *Popular Romances of the West of England*, 1865, 82; Wentz, *Fairy Faith*, 178.

cloud of the pisgey moths.[4] A final account from the south west of England underlines the close association between pixies and moths. A woman from the Blackdown Hills of Somerset felt a large moth brush across her brow and, as a result, found that she had received the 'pixy-sight,' which enabled her to see an old pixy man who had come to ask for her skill in nursing his sick wife.[5]

As stated, about a fifth of recorded familiars took rodent form and we will find examples of this in the faerylore too. In the Suffolk tale of Brother Mike, some faeries stealing ears of wheat from a farmer's barn do so in the guise of a swarm of "hundreds of little white mice; they all had red ears and red feet ...". In the previous Part we noticed the experience of a man on Shetland who was surrounded by trows in the shape of mice.[6] Lastly, we have a tale from Lochranza, on the Isle of Arran, which features a faery queen in amphibian form. A midwife was harvesting oats in a field when the reapers found a large and heavily pregnant yellow frog. One of the workers wanted to kill the creature but the midwife prevented this, remarking that the toad would soon benefit from someone with her skills. Soon afterwards, the midwife was taken to attend to the queen in labour under a nearby knoll.[7]

As will be seen, traditional accounts of British faeries indicate that animal form was not all unusual for them, supporting the idea that 'imps' were, in fact, just another way of referring to faery helpers.

---

4   Thoms in *Athenaeum*, no.1041, 1055; Harris, *Cornish Saints and Sinners,* 1907, c.20.

5   Mathews, *Tales of the Blackdown Borderland,* 59

6   Lois Fison, *Brother Mike,* 1893; Francis Young, *Suffolk Fairylore,* 130.

7   Robertson, 'Folklore from the West of Ross-shire,' *Transactions of the Gaelic Society of Inverness,* vol.26, 1905, 271; MacDougall & Calder, *Folk Tales and Fairylore,* 271.

Help from Familiars

Witches' familiars were sent on various missions by their keepers. One Victorian authority described how witches were frequently "mere victims of their own vindictive feelings and found ready instruments in certain imps, of a very equivocal character, to wreak their malice on man and beast."[1]

As I have already described, a bargain existed between imps and witches. In return for performing errands for their keepers, the familiars expected shelter (they were often kept in lined boxes) and they demanded food, such as the witch's own blood or milk. In an anomalous example from Rochford in Essex, a suspected witch called Hart was alleged to have grown white poppies in her garden 'for her imps.' Why they should want flowers is not immediately comprehensible, but perhaps the idea arose from the fact that faeries have, increasingly, become closely associated with flowers and other plants. There is, for instance, a story from Tavistock describing pixies who loved to spend their nights in an old woman's tulip bed – and, in turn, the flowers thrived from their presence. After the woman died, the flower plot was converted to growing herbs by the next residents of the cottage and the aggrieved pixies blighted it.[2]

Inevitably, the evidence of the witch trials predominantly involves cases where familiars had been despatched to exact personal revenge for the witch. They did this in numerous ways – by killing people or their livestock, or at least by making them ill and by destroying crops – but they could inflict other lesser nuisances and, even, perform more useful roles. Margaret Benet of Bacton used familiars to torment her neighbours – for instance,

---

1 T. Wright, *Narratives of Sorcery & Magic,* vol.1, 1851, 281.
2 Craven Mason, *Essex – Its Forest, Folk & Folklore,* 112; A. Bray, *A Description of the Part of Devonshire Bordering on the Tamar and Tavy,* 1836, 190.

by getting a cow to headbutt Goody Garnham; Alice Wright of Hitcham confessed that she had employed her four imps over a period of sixty years to trouble her neighbours' cattle. Anne Randall of Lavenham used her imp Jacob, a blue cat, to take away bushes that a Mr Coppinger had laid around his land. Clearly, this was some dispute over enclosure, but the ability to interfere with field boundaries recalls the tricks played by pixies in misleading people at night. Curiously, John Bonham, a hedger of Sutton in Norfolk, used his mole imp to bewitch some bullocks that had broken through a hedge he had newly laid.[3]

Faith Mills of Fressingfield had three birds as her familiars; the mischief they had caused included knocking John Wolnose off his horse into a pond and bewitching a Mr Aldus' cart so that it wouldn't move. Alice Manfield of Thorpe-le-Soken did exactly the same, sending two of her imps to stop John Sayer's cart moving. Interference with horses and wagons was, apparently, a common witch trait: various other cases from Sussex and Hampshire could be cited. Readers may also recall from Part One the Lancashire sprite called 'Old Skrat' whose habit was to leap onto carts and stop them.[4]

As stated, in numerous cases, imps were used to strike down cattle. Often, we don't learn their exact fate, other than to know that they were 'bewitched to death' but we are sometimes told that they 'languished' whilst two cases are particularly detailed and informative. For example, a young man from Denford in Northamptonshire confessed that he sent one of his imps against a Mr Cockes' cattle; they were made to violently run away from Cockes, foaming at the mouth. Jane Ruceulver of Powstead sent

---

3 Cases can be found, for example in C. L'Estrange-Ewen, *Witch Hunting & Witch Trials,* 1929; S. Hickey & G. Quaife, *Livestock Death, Plant Ingestion & Witchcraft in 16th & 17th Century England,* University of New England thesis, 1989, c.5; Exeter University, *East Anglia & the Hopkins Trials – a County Guide 1645–47* and *East Anglian Witch Trials,* Appendix 2. For Bonham, see Porter, *Folklore of East Anglia,* 140.

4 For Hampshire & Sussex see S. Cooper, *A Sussex Book of Witch Legends,* 44–47 & 49–59.

her imp, Touch, to kill a bullock which he did by striking it on the right side. This, of course, sounds very like a beast struck by an elf-bolt; the sickening referred to is a typical symptom of an elf-struck animal.[5]

Jane Linstead of Holsworth had three imps called Meg, Joan and Nag; she sent one of these against a local baker to hinder the baking of his bread. This reminds me especially of the Welsh *tylwyth teg,* who also engage in such malicious pranks. In much the same fashion, Margaret Grevell of Thorpe in Essex affected two brewings by John Carter, so that they had to be thrown away. Around Britain, it was common to appease the faeries or protect the vats with charms so that they would not interfere in beermaking: from the Western Isles of Scotland, for example, we hear of a man who annoyed his domestic brownie by reading the bible whilst ale was brewing – in revenge for which, the brownie spoiled two brews. Thirdly, Mary Bacon of Chattisham sent her two imps to kill crows; curiously, another Welsh faery report reveals the hostility of the *tylwyth teg* to rooks: a man was rewarded for destroying a nest in a tree near a faery ring.[6]

Much more benign was the case of Margery Sparham, from Mendham in mid-Suffolk, who confessed to using her imp to protect her husband, who was a soldier fighting in the Civil War. This case mirrors that of the brownie of the MacNeills of Cariskey, which accompanied a family member to war and protected him from harm.[7] Such cases are, of course, purely personal and very small-scale interventions in the course of the conflict. Some witches seem to have been much more ambitious. We heard earlier about the Bury St Edmunds' witches who sent their 'hags' to assist the Royalists in battle. Two other Suffolk women did the

---

5 On elf shot, see my *Darker Side of Faery,* 2021, chapter 1.

6 J. Ceredig Davies, *Folklore,* 135; M. Lewes, *Queer Side,* 114; Porter, *Folklore of East Anglia,* 76; M. Martin, *A Description of the Western Isles of Scotland,* 1716, 391–392; Rhys, *Celtic Folklore,* 140–141; on brewing, see my *Darker Side of Faery,* c.5.

7 A. Campbell, *Records of Argyll,* 1885, 375.

same: Mary Everard of Metfield despatched her imps to assist the king's nephew, Prince Rupert, and Anne Barker of Glemham ordered her imp to go to her son so that he could take it to King Charles.

The mention of brownies on the last paragraph reminds us of the practical help that they (along with boggarts and hobs) typically give in human households and on farms. Imps can perform the same functions. See, for example, the case of the Victorian wizard, or cunning man, George Pickingill, from Canewdon in Essex, who claimed that his imps could harvest a field of grain for him in half an hour, whilst he relaxed and supervised with a pipe of tobacco. In the same manner, Jack Kent, of Kentchurch in Herefordshire, had an imp the size of a fly that he kept in a hollow at the end of a walking stick. He simply laid down the stick next to any task that needed completing and it would be done, whilst he played his fiddle.[8]

Imps could seek to directly enrich witches, as well as performing chores for them. For example, Alice Wright of Hitcham in Suffolk had over a period of sixty years kept four imps, a lamb, a grey buzzard and two little boys. The larger of the pair one day, with a loud, hoarse voice, had advised her to "go into the field and she should have money and should never misse or want anything." Alice had acted on this advice, but found nothing. The same was the case with Katherine Tooly, from the Suffolk village of Westleton, who was told by her imp about a "bushel of rusty money" hidden in a closet – but he never brought it to her nor guided her to its discovery. These two failures notwithstanding, guiding mortals to buried treasure (or, at least, teasing them with the knowledge of its existence) was a very common faery trait. Even more frequently, faeries will give coins to favoured humans – and imps will do the same. Joan Wallis of Keyston in Cambridgeshire was brought money by her imps, as was a witch

---

8   See, for example, S. Cooper, *A Sussex Book of Witch Legends*, 2020, 89 or S. Kent, *Folklore of Essex*, 2005, 45; Westwood & Simpson, *Lore of the Land*, 324.

from Faversham. Her familiar, a little dog called Bun, regularly brought her small coins (6d or 1/-). Some imps instead provided their keepers with wealth in kind. John Winnick, a farm labourer at Molesworth (near Keyston) employed his imp to get a maid servant to steal food for him from her master's house. Elizabeth Francis, tried at Chelmsford in 1566, was helped by her familiar – a cat named Satan – to gain modest wealth in the form of a flock of eighteen black and white sheep (although these eventually just disappeared from the field in which she had grazed them). The same familiar assisted a friend, Agnes Waterhouse, with the farm chore of slaughtering a pig – just as a brownie might.[9]

Fortunately for the witches' victims, imps could be resisted and defeated through the Christian faith. Katherine Tooly of Westleton tried to use her imp to harm the church minister Hugh Driver but failed because of the strength of his faith in his god. John Walsh told his interrogators that saying the Lord's prayer and the creed daily was a guaranteed protection against witches and many readers will be aware of the widespread use of blessings, signs of the cross and pages from the bible or prayer books as equally effective measures against faeries. Other charms effective against faeries were also effective against witches and, one imagines, their imps: for example, St John's Wort placed in a window was believed in Essex to keep witches out.[10]

Although, as Ronald Hutton has characterised it, there was generally a "domestic or nurturing relationship" with a witch, some imps could prove to be troublesome to their keepers as well. Elizabeth Chandler of Keyston admitted to her interrogators that she had been pestered by imps and spirits for many years, although she had never encouraged or sought them. Elizabeth Finch of Wattisham had likewise been plagued by imps in the

---

9 Wright, *Narratives of Sorcery & Magic,* vol.2, 1851, 154. On faery gifts of money & treasure, see my *How Things Work in Faery,* Green Magic, 2021.

10 Craven Mason, *Essex: Its Forest, Folk & Folklore,*114; for charms, see my *Darker Side of Faery,* 2021, chapter 5.

form of dogs for a period of over twenty years, in one instance turning her out of the chair she sat in. Alice Wright, mentioned already, often refused to cooperate with her imps and then was "much troubled and tormented and in extreame paine." These cases might be compared to examples where domestic boggarts have harassed their human household with their incessant pranks or a Welsh incident in which faeries invaded a woman's cottage, besieging and tormenting her.[11]

Just like faeries (see Part Four) imps could be too fast to catch. A rag and bone man at Horseheath in Cambridgeshire was asked by the local witch where he was going. He told her to mind her own business and went on his way. After about half a mile, he realised that he was being followed by one of her imp-mice, which was running along behind him in the hedgerow. He gave chase, but the faster he ran, the imp would gain speed and stay ahead of him until they got back to the witch's home. Equally, they could simply vanish – just like faeries – melting into solid objects such as a floor.[12]

Finally, it could prove very hard to get rid of imps. Burning was the usual method tried, although it is not always successful. One witch, living at West Wickham in Cambridgeshire at the start of the last century, tried to dispose of hers by roasting them to death in her oven. They shrieked so much she eventually had to relent and remove them; they were eventually buried with her. The two bat imps of the mother and daughter witches at Loddon were thrown on the fire in their box and destroyed after the older woman's death. The significance of these incidents is that faeries too are regarded as generally immortal and indestructible, although occasionally they have been killed, for example by fire.

11 Hutton, *The Witch,* 272; on boggarts, see my *Beyond Faery,* 2020, 132 & 175; W. Stanley, 'Folklore Superstition in Anglesey,' *Notes & Queries,* 4th series, vol.9, 1871, 255.

12 C.E. Parsons, 'Notes on Cambridgeshire Witchcraft,' *Proceedings of the Cambridge Antiquarian Society,* vol.19, 1915, 34; Westwood & Simpson, *Lore of the Land,* 678; Wright, *Narratives,* vol.2, 146 & 174.

The diametrical opposite solution was used to dispose of the imps belonging to Jabez Few of Willingham after his death in 1920. His nephew stood in running water holding the familiars until the creatures ran off and a vanished. Exactly the same happened with the imp belonging to Anne West, from Rivenhall in Essex. A man tried to drown the familiar, which looked like a black rabbit, in a spring, but in disappeared as soon as he put in under the water. In folklore, a guaranteed defence against faeries can be to cross a flowing stream – over which they will not be able to pass in pursuit.[13]

---

13 E. Porter, *Cambridgeshire Customs & Folklore,* 5 & 176 and *Folklore of East Anglia,* 149; Westwood & Simpson, *Lore of the Land,* 507; Wright, *Narratives,* vol.2, 149. See too my *Faery Lifecycle,* 2021, c.5.

Faery Skin Tones

The preceding section demonstrated how imps can behave in many ways just like faeries, yet don't look as we'd expect. Sometimes, though, the faeries themselves may not look the way we'd expect.

Earlier we considered the testimony of John Walsh, the Dorset man accused of sorcery. As well as telling his inquisitors about faery familiars, he also had something else of great interest to say about the faeries that he met. According to the court record, Walsh explained that:

> "There be iii kindes of feries, white, greene and black ... Whereof (he sayeth) the blacke feries be the woorst."

Our first reaction at reading this may be mystification, but the most likely explanation for Walsh's statement would seem to be that he is referring to the faeries' clothing. This would certainly not be an unreasonable conclusion, for numerous sources support it. Consider, for example, William Byrd's 1588 madrigal, which begins "Though Amarillis daunce in green/ like Fayrie Queene." In 1696, the suspected Cornish witch Ann Jeffries was reported to have met "six Persons of a small Stature, all clothed in green, which she call'd Fairies." From the nineteenth century, we have records that the faery folk of the Lincolnshire fens were called the 'green coaties,' whilst those of Lancashire were simply the 'greenies.'[1]

Bearing this in mind, we might well arrive at a similar understanding of other contemporary phrases – for example, in Gascoigne's play *Buggbears* when we are told that there are "sondry names by which we do call them [i.e. the faeries]; some

---

1 See Bowker, *Goblin Tales of Lancashire*, 1878.

are called ... the whyte and red fearye." In the same way, in William Camden's 1586 survey of the British Isles, *Britannia,* we learn of a used by cunning women in Ireland to treat the sickness called 'esane':

> "Against all maladies and mischiefs whatsoever the women have effectual enchantments or charms ... [If a man has a fall and becomes sick] there is sent a woman skilful in that kind unto the said place, and there she saith on this wise: 'I call thee ... from the East and West, South and North, from the forests, woods, rivers, meeres, the wilde wood-fayries, white, red, black etc ...'. Then returneth she home unto the sick party, to try whither it be the disease called Esane, which they are of opinion is sent by the Fairies ... and so giveth more certain judgment of the disease than many of our physicians can."[2]

However, there is a possibility that the colours mentioned might not refer to the faeries' clothes but to their complexions. Consider, for instance, Ben Jonson's reference to the "finest olive-coloured spirits," as well, more vaguely, to "white fays."

Jonson's usage might leave us in doubt as to how to interpret poet Thomas Heywood's mention of 'White Nymphs' or James Hart's intriguing reference to "the white devils, the Faries, or rather (as they say they were usually to be seene) the greene Divells [who] were wont to pinch the maids in the night time, if all were not cleane in the House."[3]

How were Walsh and others using their colour adjectives? How did they think of the faeries they described? Other contemporary examples of usage will help us understand what was being said. Isobel Gowdie, from Auldearn near Nairn in North East Scotland,

---

2 Gascoigne, *Buggbears,* 1565, line 47; Camden, *Britannia* vol.4, 470.
3 Jonson, *The Gypsies Metamorphosis,* 1621; *The Sad Shepherd*; Heywood, *Hierarchie of Blessed Angels,* 507; Hart, *Klinike,* 1633, 364.

was accused of witchcraft in 1662. Examined on these charges, she described the Devil as a "blak ... man." By way of contrast, familiar spirits that he appointed to assist her coven of witches were all said by her to have been *clothed* in grass and sea green, yellow, black and dun. Isobel appears to have made a careful distinction between colour of dress and physical colour. Likewise, Janet Trall, accused of witchcraft at Perth in May 1623: she witnessed a faery band "who appeared some of them red, some of them grey, and riding on horses." The principal amongst them was a "bonny white man, riding upon a grey horse." Elsewhere in her testimony, she recounted how the fairies had once come to her "clad in green." Trall, just like Isobel Gowdie, seemed perfectly able to distinguish between the colour of the individuals and of their garments.[4]

In these examples, the accused individuals seem to have clearly differentiated between clothing and skin colour – and to have accepted that the latter might be quite non-human. Dr Minor White Latham was an American authority on Tudor literature, especially the plays of the period, who argued in the study, *Elizabethan Fairies* (1930), that the writers and audiences of the time did indeed hold conceptions about the colour of faeries radically different to our own. Latham noted the fact that the Tudors and Stuarts loved performing as faes in masques and plays, and to do so they put on masks. So, in *The Buggbears*, there's reference to spirits played by actors in "visars like devills," to going "a-sprityng with this face and that" and "buggbears with vysardes." Latham argued that these masks weren't just part of the theatrical spectacle, but actually reflected popular conceptions about what she called the 'complexion' of the faeries – their skin colour.

---

4 *Pitcairn's Ancient Criminal Trials in Scotland*, vol.3(2), 603, 606 & 610; *Extracts from the Presbytery Book of Strathbogie*, 1843, xi.

A good demonstration of this may be found in Shakespeare's *Merry Wives of Windsor* (1602), in which a plot is hatched to make a fool of Sir John Falstaff by having some children dressed as faeries scare him. Mrs Anne Page decides her daughter Nan and some others shall "dress / Like urchins, ouphs and fairies, green and white." Nan is to be the faery queen in a white silk dress and it's very evident from the line just quoted that the others will be wearing green and white too. Mrs Page's friend, Mrs Ford, then says "I'll go buy them vizards (masks)." In a slightly later scene, in which the women go over their plans again and agree that the children should be "mask'd and vizarded." They'll be in disguise, with their faces covered. So, when Falstaff is confronted by queen Nan and she calls forth her "Fairies, black, grey, green and white," there's support for Latham's suggestion that these colours relate *not* (just) to their clothes but to the colour of their masks (that is, their faces) as well.[5]

Further support for the idea that faeries had strangely coloured faces comes from the text of a masque performed for Queen Elizabeth at Woodstock in 1575. The entertainment began with the monarch being approached by the 'Queen of Fayry,' who declared that her love for Elizabeth had inspired her to leave her woodland retreat and had "caused me transforme my face/ and, in your hue, to come before your eyne/ now white, then blacke, your frend the fayery Queene." Black and white were the colours of the English queen, yet at the same time it did not appear to be considered odd that her supernatural counterpart might have a black face.

Bearing these examples in mind, we might wish to reassess other cases. Reginald Scot in his *Discourse Concerning the Nature and Substance of Devils and Spirits* mentioned "white spirits and black spirits, grey spirits and red spirits;" in *Macbeth* the three witches meet with Hecate to summon up "Black spirits."

---

5 *Merry Wives of Windsor,* Act IV, scenes 4 & 6; Act V, scene 5.

A masque performed in February 1618 at Cole-Orton Hall in Leicestershire featured a character asking Puck about "ye faries, those little ring-leaders, those white and blew faries." In his play, *Monsieur Thomas,* John Fletcher has a character attempting to conjure spirits of earth and air, whom he addresses thus:

> "Be thou ghost that cannot rest, or a shadow of the blest,
> Be thou black or white or green, be thou heard or seen."[6]

Finally, the accused witch Joan Willimot, mentioned earlier, was told by her faery familiar Pretty that the Earl of Rutland's son had been "stricken with a white spirit." This, especially, suggests that the spirit was a ghostly white – and, indeed, the son sickened and died in due course.

Where the Tudor and Stuart texts are highly suggestive, later folklore accounts are quite clear that faeries may be strangely coloured. Several Welsh witnesses have affirmed that the *tylwyth teg* not only wear white but have white skin, hair *and* eyes. The Shetland trows, meanwhile, have green teeth, red eyes and yellowy skins. Later reports, therefore, of 'green women' and 'green folk' may be just that. All in all, then, it seems there is some quite convincing evidence that British people of the early modern period conceived of their fays as being quite alien in appearance – red, green, blue, grey, jet black and snow white.[7]

One last remark. Throughout the book, we have noted the fluidity of terminology – spirit, faery, devil and so on. Recalling John Walsh's statement about different coloured faeries at the start of this section, note the 1677 comments of one Scottish church minister, Robert Knox, regarding spirits that:

---

6 Scot, *Discourse,* c.33; Fletcher, *Monsieur Thomas,* c.1637, Act V, scene 9.
7 See Wherry, 'Miscellaneous Notes from Monmouthshire,' *Folklore,* vol.16, 63; Simpson, *Folklore of the Welsh Borders,* 73; W. Marwick, *Folklore of Orkney & Shetland,* 1975, 42.

"the vulgar call white deviles, which possibly have neither so much power nor malice as the black ones have, which served our great grandfathers under the names of Brouny, and Robin Goodfellow, and, to this day, make dayly service to severals in quality of familiars."[8]

Knox was discussing a recent witch trial in Renfrewshire. This led him to remark, too, how devils were believed to shapeshift or to appear as incubi and succubi. He also commented that one of the witches in the case may have been instructed in her skills by supernatural beings, which he called "changelings of heaven, aerial spirites." These are the white devils mentioned above which are, he suggested, scared of the black kind. Knox went on to tell the story of a woman living on the Borders with England who was always accompanied by benign spirit, "in the shape of a little old fellow." When the pair were once out riding, a "big unshapely spirit" appeared before them and the small man jumped up behind his mistress on her horse and clasped her about her waist for comfort and protection. This timidity might well be thought to fit better with a faery than with a demon.[9]

CONCLUSIONS

All the scattered examples of animal faeries may seem insignificant on their own but, put together and considered in the context of the witch trials, they actually suggest that in Tudor and Stuart England the parallels between imps and faeries were much closer than we might initially suspect. If this is correct, and 'imp' was – in fact – just another way of describing a faery, then

---

8 R. Law, *Memorialls*, 1818, lxxvi.
9 Knox in Robert Laws, *Memorialls*, lxxiv–lxxvii; the phrase 'changelings of the air' is a quotation from John Dryden, *Tyrannic Love,* 1669, Act IV, scene 1. It refers to some conjured spirits of the air that have power over love.

our view of faery nature may have to be revised. It would appear that it was very common to encounter faeries in purely animal form. This seems a radical departure from our contemporary understanding of Faery, but it should not be rejected for this reason alone: as we've just seen, the idea that faeries had very different skin colours was also accepted by people at the time.[10] Just like the animal imps, with the passage of time, we seem to have forgotten this; perhaps we need to be more open and flexible.

Why has the animal form of faeries been lost to memory? It could be the very fact of the witch trials that contributed to this. As author Francis Young wrote, "in the agonised confessions of Suffolk's accused witches, we are witnessing the process by which fairy belief was crushed and demonised by the weight of Puritan theology." Perhaps it simply became too dangerous to recognise faeries as having common animal forms. It is very likely that many of the old and single women caught up in the witch-hunts had no supernatural contacts or interests at all and that the cats and other creatures labelled as their imps were no more than companion creatures that they kept for company (or, even, simply happened to be present in their homes). If pets could be mistaken as faeries, popular culture may well have suppressed that link for reasons of self-protection and preservation.[11]

---

10 See too my *Fayerie,* 2019.
11 Young, *Suffolk Fairylore,* 75.

Final Conclusions

Nowadays, many people automatically imagine faeries as being small, feminine and winged creatures, perhaps wearing tiaras and carrying wands. This appears to be the product of works such as Cicely Mary Barker's *Flower Fairy* books for (as I have frequently pointed out) the faeries of authentic British tradition do not look anything like this. Nonetheless, their appearance is still reasonably conventional. The faeries of folklore resemble small human beings and dress in familiar clothes whilst engaging – for the most part – in everyday human activities.

However, as I have tried to stress in the preceding pages, what it has become conventional to expect today need not be what our predecessors expected or encountered. They seem to have been much more at ease with the idea that 'Faery' was a broad term that encompassed many different types of supernatural being. Their mental image of a faery was not restricted to a tiny human being, but could include vividly coloured creatures and animals (amongst others). Their motion and their interactions with us could differ quite markedly from what we tend to expect.

Secondly, as I said at the start, we've been concerned here with investigating the boundaries of faery – those limits of our understanding and preconceptions where 'faery' shades into demon, ghost and monster. Often these grey areas are skated over; here, we have confronted – at least admitted – them.

This book, therefore, presents readers with a number of mysterious and surprising visions of Faery, and challenges them to think differently about the entire subject. It may – in fact – be richer and more surprising than we had already assumed. We accept that faeries are magical beings, but have we have tended to limit the scope of those magical powers. Perhaps we need to reassess the scope of their glamour.

www.ingramcontent.com/pod-product-compliance
Lightning Source LLC
Chambersburg PA
CBHW070805100426

42742CB00012B/2251